M000013379

HIT IT!

YOUR VICTORY MAY JUST BE ONE "HIT IT" AWAY!

by Kristi Overton Johnson

ENDORSEMENTS

Deuteronomy 6:5 says, "You must love the Lord your God with all your heart, all your soul, and all your strength." Pursuing this verse is an adventure that promises to be a journey of a lifetime. For Kristi and for me, much of the journey has been experienced on the water. It is my pleasure to encourage you to read this most compelling story of Kristi's journey and how it has shaped her. **Don M. (Bubba) Cathy, Executive Vice President, Chick-fil-A**

I know I've made my share of mistakes in my career and in my life. Whether you are seeking a win on the football field, race track or in the game of life, how you respond to adversity often defines whether or not you will be a success. In Hit It! Kristi provides a testimony of determination, perseverance, and humility that we can all benefit from. **Joe Gibbs, Pro Football Hall of Fame Coach, 3-time Super Bowl Champion and 3-time NASCAR Sprint Cup Series Champion as owner of Joe Gibbs Racing**

Water-skiing isn't quite the same as walking on water, but if you've ever watched a skier glide and then bump across the waves, you have a picture of the Christian life. In these pages, you'll grasp the analogies as champion skier Kristi Overton Johnson grabs hold of the rope and shouts to the boat's driver, "Hit it!" (which means that she is ready for action). She comes up out of the water clinging to the lifeline, pulled by the strength and power of the boat's engine. This is the story of how Christ, our Captain, will throw us The Lifeline and connect us to His power, enabling us to maneuver stormy waves and bring us into the exhilaration of knowing He is at the controls. Hold on for life and follow Him; grasp the rope and bellow out… "Hit it!" **Franklin Graham, President and CEO Samaritan's Purse, Billy Graham Evangelistic Association**

I've been a water-skier most of my life. I've been blessed to spend time with some of the world's best skiers, and I always love hearing their stories. Let's face it: this is a hard sport! There are no soft landings when you hit the water traveling in excess of 60 mph! In Hit It!, former world record holder Kristi Overton Johnson shares her trials, challenges, and victories from a lifetime on the water to show you how your biggest win might be just one effort away. **Dave Ramsey, *New York Times* best-selling author and nationally syndicated radio show host**

I am most impressed with the way Kristi's passion for the presence of God is communicated on every page of this book. The depth of character that was formed in her life as she hungered for Jesus above all else helped guide her on her journey to repurpose her gifts and talents and the dreams she held dear. The love of God she now emanates, even in her writings, transcends denominational lines and will bless readers of every station, calling, and experience. Read this book, launch out into the deep, and fall in love with Jesus all over again. **Erlita Renner, Partner Care Director, Rick Renner Ministries**

Additional Published Works by Kristi Overton Johnson

Making the Cut (Devotional Tract)

Running the Course: Becoming a Champion in God's Eyes (Hardback)

On the Go with Kristi (Audio Devotional CD)

Living Victoriously (Paperback Devotional)

Victorious Living (Magazine)

Visit www.kojministries.org to purchase these works.

HIT IT!

Hit It!

Copyright © 2015 by Kristi Overton Johnson

All rights reserved. No part of this book may be reproduced or transmitted in any form or by any means, electronic or mechanical, including photocopying and recording, or by any information storage and retrieval system, without permission in writing from the author.

For latest contact information, visit www.kojministries.org.

Unless otherwise noted, all scripture is taken from the Holy Bible, New Living Translation. Copyright© 1996, 2004, 2007 by Tyndale House Foundation. Used by permission of Tyndale House Publishers Inc., Carol Stream, Illinois 60188. All rights reserved.

Scripture marked NIV is taken from the Holy Bible, New International Version®, NIV® Copyright © 1973, 1978, 1984, 2011 by Biblica, Inc.® Used by permission. All rights reserved worldwide.

Scripture marked RSV is taken from the Revised Standard Version of the Bible. Copyright © 1946, 1952, and 1971, the Division of Christian Education of the National Council of the Churches of Christ in the United States of America. Used by permission. All rights reserved.

ISBN: 069222940X

ISBN 13: 9780692229408

DEDICATION

This book is dedicated to anyone who has ever fallen in life. May you discover newfound purpose, hope, and worth, and the courage to rise up again and again, remembering that your victory may be just one "hit it!" away.

ACKNOWLEDGMENTS

To my faithful, loving husband, Tim. Thank you for standing by my side and being willing to love me, even in the midst of my pain and my mistakes. God gave me such an incredible gift in you.

To my amazing children—Ty, Dalton, and Ivy. I am so proud of each one of you. I thank God for bringing us together from across the world. Always be willing to say, "Hit it, God!" every day of your lives. He has great plans for you. Trust His plan and trust His heart, even when you don't understand it. God's love will never fail you.

To my dad and mom. Thank you for introducing me to the little yet powerful phrase, "Hit it." As I learned to say these two words to the boat driver over and over again, they led me to victory and forever impacted my life. Now, I pray, they will continue to impact the lives of others as they learn the power of saying "Hit it" in their daily lives. Thank you for spurring me on to victory, both on the water and in life. Words cannot express how grateful I am for your love.

To my brother, Michael. Thank you for your support and love throughout the years. I love you and am so proud of the man of God you have become. Not only do I call you brother, I call you friend.

To my dear friend, Jackie. Thank you for being a faithful friend and training partner for nearly fifteen years. You pushed me to say "Hit it!" on the water and helped me become a champion. I owe much of my success to you.

And finally, to my Lord and Savior Jesus Christ. Thank You for picking me up time and time again, for loving me, and for teaching me Your ways. This book is a testimony of Your faithfulness.

Lord…all [I] have accomplished is really from you.
Isaiah 26:12

Champions aren't people who never fall. They are people who choose to get up time and time again and press on toward their victory!

TABLE OF CONTENTS

FOREWORD

And you will know the truth, and the truth will set you free.
PSALM 34:8

My fellow reader, welcome to the well-known triumphs but little-known inner struggles of one of the world's greatest sports champions of all times—Kristi Overton Johnson.

When Kristi reached out to me, asking if I'd take the time to read her book, I told her to send it my way. I was in need of a new read and was interested to learn a bit more about her life. Little did I know how this powerfully honest and humble autobiography would move me. Not only is it super exciting, but it is extremely edifying.

Personally, I want to commend and thank Kristi for taking the time to do what very few people, much less public champions, would be willing to do—she let us in! She opened the doorway of her soul and invited the world to learn from her past failures and triumphs.

Let's face it. Most of today's champions won't allow family—much less the general public—into that secret little closet in their heart of hearts where they, like the rest of us, systematically hide their real feelings, failures, and fears. In the more-plastic-than-real world where we live, most champions parade up and down their playing fields, gyms, stages, and even waters, flaunting their great deeds but never once sharing their misdeeds. They would die if anyone could get inside their soul's inner chamber and see how hollow and hurting they really are.

Thank God, for our sakes, Kristi chose to be different and to do the hard thing—the humbling thing—something very few people would ever drum up the courage to do. She got real.

Why did she do it? I believe it was out of obedience. She wrote this thrilling autobiography for us because her Master Coach whispered to her heart, "Baby, tell it all!"

He knew many would read this book and through her transparency, would be drawn closer to Him and find that place of peace that took Kristi years to find! And I think that is Kristi's greatest desire, too.

The true champion in her wants you and me to not only meet but to know intimately the Lord of her life—Captain Jesus—so that we, too, can experience His love, peace, joy, and victory. Without a doubt, Kristi wants to encourage us to *let go and let God* take over the controls of our lives so that we can experience a life of true worth and purpose.

She wants to encourage us to rise up and trust God enough to say, "Okay, Lord, hit it! Take me wherever You desire me to go," as she knows that only then can we truly experience what every champion desires—victory.

World champions are plentiful. *Word* champions are rare. Kristi is both! It's time for us to dive in…

"Hit it!"

Dr. Bobby Joiner has been involved in local teen and prison ministries, as well as traveling around the world singing and teaching God's Word. Since 2007, he has enjoyed being the tour pastor for the contemporary Christian group, NewSong, and for the world's largest music tour, Winter Jam. His personal ministry is nondenominational and stresses an eternal relationship and daily fellowship with God through His Son, Jesus Christ.

PREFACE

When I entered into this writing project a couple of years ago, I had no idea what lay ahead of me. Initially, as with any new project, I was filled with passion and excitement. As I sat and wrote daily, words just poured out of me. I had every chapter laid out on paper and organized in my mind.

"This isn't so hard," I thought. "I'll be done with this in no time!"

Then, about four months down the road, life hit. Trials came in various forms, and transitions abounded. One of the first things I set aside was this book.

Months went by, and then over a year passed. As God brought new responsibilities and changes into my life, my attention was forced to go elsewhere. In the midst of it all, I felt no desire to write. I just couldn't pick up where I had left off. It wasn't the time; nor did I have the time.

I could sense in the depths of my heart that God was doing something. He was at work, teaching me more about His grace, love, peace, and provision. And even greater still, He was reaching into my heart, healing my innermost wounds, and bringing to light so much that had been hidden. As I look back now, I can see that during that time, God was rewriting the book I had imagined in my heart and mind.

In January 2014, as I was ministering in Russia at the orphanage where my husband and I had adopted our two youngest children almost a decade before, I felt the Lord urging me to start writing again. It was time to finish what I had started. As I sat in obedience, the words began to flow once more. And oh, how different the story that was being written! Because of my experiences and the faithfulness of God to see me through, I simply wasn't the same person that I had been when I began this project.

Over the course of time—from when I had started this book until I picked it up again—the Lord has taught me much. He has opened my eyes to incredible truths and poured a measure of joy and peace into my life. Even now as I finalize the project with the typing of this preface, He continues to teach me. It's so tempting to want to share these newest nuggets of truth. But I know that if I do that, this book will continue forever—for the teachings of the Lord, if our hearts are open, are never-ending!

So, for now, I stop, trusting that the words that follow are the exact words the Lord desires for this book. And the rest? Well, they will just have to wait until God prompts my heart to write the next book.

I have no idea how God will use the words in these pages. One thing is for sure—this book will serve as a timeless reminder to my own self of God's faithful and unfailing love. And when I am weak and tired and maybe even aching a bit…it will give me that kick in the rear I need to spur me on to say "Hit it!" one more time, as I'm reminded that victory may be just one "hit it!" away. I pray it does the same for you.

Before we embark on this journey, let me explain how the book is organized. Each chapter provides an intimate glimpse into my life story, with all its twists and turns, from the time I put on my first pair of water skis until now. At the end of each chapter, there is a section called: "Something to Think About." This part of the book provides you an opportunity to take the insights and lessons from my life story and apply it to your own life. This thought-provoking section makes for a perfect personal or small group study.

INTRODUCTION

Taste and see that the Lord is good.
Oh, the joys of those who take refuge in him!
PSALM 34:8

One day as I was walking down the hallway of my high school, I heard a comment I will never forget.

"Hey, you!" a tall, athletic boy called out to me. I stopped and turned around.

"Have you ever fallen off those water skis?" Evidently, this boy had heard about my career as a professional water-skier.

"Of course," I replied. "Every day."

"You're no good!" he taunted and began to walk away.

Knowing this young man was on the basketball team, I couldn't resist asking him a question of my own.

"Hey!" I called out. He stopped and turned around. "Have you ever missed a shot in basketball?"

He looked like a deer in headlights. "Uh…yeah," he stammered.

"Well, I guess you're no good either."

We both stared at each other for a moment and then broke into smiles. This young man knew I had made a point.

Everyone falls. Any athlete who is committed to push himself to learn a new feat or face an opponent will make a mistake at some point and miss the mark. It's part of the process. Very few get it right the first time, and no one gets it right all the time.

During my thirty-year career as a water-skier, I fell flat on my face over and over again. Sometimes these falls were gentle, resulting in a slow descent into the water. Other times they hurt so bad, I thought I'd never recover. Some of the falls were a result of my own mistakes, while others were due to equipment failure, inclement conditions, or another person's actions.

1

In the midst of all these falls, however, something amazing happened. I became a champion. At first it was on local, state, and regional levels, but then I reached the national level. Then, after years of commitment and perseverance, success came at a professional and international level as I captured every water-ski championship title and held the world record in women's slalom for eighteen years.

Stop for a moment and think about what I just said. *In the midst of my falls, I became a world champion.* Isn't it encouraging to know that despite failures, someone can move forward to claim victory at the highest level? So often people think falls prevent success; the reality, however, is that falls are stepping stones to the top of the podium, whether in sports or in life.

As I think back to my incredible journey on the water, I can say with all certainty that my falls made the greatest impact on my career.

How?

With each fall came a new opportunity—if I was willing—to learn. Each fall presented a chance for me to master a new skill, to grow in my abilities as an athlete, and most importantly, to develop character.

Champions aren't people who never fall or fail. Rather, they are people who choose to get up after each fall, brush themselves off (or in my case, dry herself off), and say "Hit it!" In the world of water-skiing, "Hit it!" is the command the skier gives to the boat driver signifying his or her readiness to go and willingness to try again. A skier who commits to push past their pride, frustrations, excuses, insecurities, doubts, and fears to say "Hit it!" is a skier who is on their way to victory. The same is true in our spiritual lives.

As a Christian, remembering this truth brings me great comfort. I've made a lot of mistakes in my life—we all have. I've fallen short of God's perfect standard every day, just like I fell on the water for thirty years! Yet, as I look at the lives of God's champions in the Bible, I find an incredibly comforting truth: God uses people who fall. God uses people who make mistakes.

Take a look at the lives of Abraham, Sarah, David, Jonah, Noah, Moses, Paul, Peter, and Rahab, to name a few. These people weren't perfect. They experienced fear, guilt, doubt, shame, pride, anger, jealousy, and some even lived openly immoral lives. They spoke harsh words, lied, acted rashly, and even committed murder. Yet God used them.

If there is one thing the above lives illustrate, it's that God isn't looking for perfect people. He isn't looking for those who have it all together or who under no circumstances make mistakes. He'd never find them! Rather, God is looking for persevering, passionate people. People who are humble enough to admit their mistakes, listen to God, learn from Him, and move forward despite their weaknesses. God is looking for people who will say "Hit it!" over and over again.

Do you like doughnuts? I know, that's a weird question in the middle of my introduction. I don't eat them often, but when I do, I want a hot Krispy Kreme doughnut. My kids and I love looking through the glass window as the dough drops onto the conveyor belt and slowly makes its way to the sugary, white coating. Those doughnuts smell and taste so good!

If you take a moment to look at them as they move along the line, you'll quickly discover that every one of them is at a different stage. Some are clumps of fresh dough, some are half-baked, others are completely cooked and being covered with a hot, delicious glaze.

Now, wipe your drool and come back to me. You and I are like these Krispy Kreme doughnuts! We are all at different levels spiritually. Some of us, as believers, are like that fresh dough. We have a lot to learn. There is a lot of transformation that needs to take place before we hit that glaze of glory! And that's okay. It's part of the process. Our Maker doesn't love us any more or any less whether we are a clump of dough or a completely covered, mouth-watering masterpiece! To Him, it's all about us staying on the conveyor belt and being transformed into what He has designed us to be.

In the following pages, I'd like to share my journey from a clump of dough to the half-baked state in which I currently find myself. Admittedly,

I have much transformation ahead of me before I reach that glaze of glory and become all that God intends. Yet already, He has taught me so much. When I've been willing to say "Hit it," He has used each stage and experience, the victories and defeats, to bring incredible, real transformation into my heart and mind that has impacted every aspect of my life including my relationships, ministries, finances, and health.

Many people think they know my story—the story of a girl who learned to water-ski at a very young age and who became a world champion; the story of a wife and mother of three children, two of whom were adopted internationally from Russia; and the story of a woman who has had the privilege of leading international ministries. Few, however, know the real story—the obstacles of physical pain, people-pleasing, perfectionism, frustrations, fears, insecurities, and doubts I have wrestled with most of my life. Obstacles that could only be overcome by making the choice to say "Hit it!"

In these pages, you will learn my real story—or should I say, God's story. It's written with complete honesty and from a heart that desires more than anything for people to learn from my mistakes, doubts, and fears. It's meant to encourage hearts to rise up out of their frustrations and setbacks and say "Hit it, God!" one more time so that they can move a little further along God's conveyor belt to that place of peace, worth, contentment, and joy.

I've tasted that place, and I'm here to tell you, it's good! It's even better than that dripping hot, sugar-coated doughnut.

Are you ready? Let's get moving.

"Hit it!"

CHAPTER I

HIT IT!

No, dear brothers and sisters, I have not achieved it,
but I focus on this one thing:
Forgetting the past and looking forward to what lies ahead. I
press on toward the goal to win the prize for which God has
called me heavenward in Christ Jesus.
PHILIPPIANS 3:13–14

"Hit it!"

"Hit what?" you may ask.

To most people, these words probably arouse images of someone hitting an object—perhaps a baseball, tennis ball, punching bag, or even a nail. The words can also be used to describe other things. For example, according to Google, some people liken the phrase "hit it" to a random act of sex between two people who have just met. Still others use it to describe taking a hit of drugs.

I bet I have your attention now, don't I?

For thirty years, however, the term "hit it" represented something entirely different for me. When I think of those two little words, I don't see an object; rather, I see a choice...a choice to try again, a choice to face an obstacle, to master a new skill, to take on a competitor, or a choice to overcome physical or emotional pain. I see two words that when spoken, enabled me to rise out of the waters of defeat to platforms of victory.

I was first introduced to the term in 1974, when I found myself floating in the Pamlico River in Bath, North Carolina. I had water skis on my feet and a rope in my hands, and I had just experienced being pulled up and down the shoreline of the shallow waters. Now it was time for me to make the decision to tell the boat driver to "hit it" and follow it out into the deep.

You would think that a four-year-old child would have some reservations about being pulled away from the safety of the shore and her family into a large, open space of water, but I didn't. There was no fear of falling, disappointing onlookers, or failing in my endeavor. There wasn't any doubt about my ability to have success. The only thing I remember about that day was my excitement about skimming across the top of the water.

To me, the choice was simple…I could either remain floating in the water, or I could give the boat driver the command to "hit it" and have some fun! So, with every bit of gusto I had in my little lungs, I gave the command, and off I went, out of the water and on to a thirty-year adventure that would take me all over the world and open unimaginable doors.

My parents first introduced me to the incredible world of water sports. It's what they did for exercise, relaxation, and family fun. My dad was what you would call a river rat. He loved hot-dogging across the water, whether on water skis or in his boat.

I vividly remember the reflection of his bright yellow ski belt as he'd do fancy tricks and kick up big sprays. I can also remember the massive wall of water coming out of the back of our jet boat. I loved it when my dad, forever a jokester, would press that magic button on the boat, releasing a giant spray that soaked whoever was in our wakes. Do I dare mention that some of those people we soaked were driving across the bridge in their cars?

From my first introduction to the sport, I loved it. It helped that my best friend, Jackie, was on this adventure with me. She and I spent a lot of time in the back of the boat as our families and friends took turns skiing. It was there that our imaginations would run wild as we invented games to entertain ourselves. One of our favorites was guarding the earth from wicked witches. We'd lie on our backs and stare up into the clouds, just waiting for a chance to blast those evil beings out of the sky with our imaginary guns.

We were thrilled when the boat came to a stop and our families gathered together for a snack. After eating a bite or two, we'd jump into the water and swim to the jump ramp, where we'd have the opportunity to slide down its steep, slick surface on our vinyl life vests. We'd do this for as long as our parents would let us, and then it was back to the boat to ski some more.

Within a few years of my learning to water-ski, it became obvious that I was excelling in the sport rather rapidly. By the age of eight, I was surpassing the abilities of my parents and challenging their coaching abilities. To keep me moving forward in my skills, my mother and I traveled to Orlando, Florida, each spring to attend a water-ski school. It was there that we learned more about the sport, both as coach and skier. With the extra knowledge we gained, our family soon found ourselves traveling across the United States, setting state, regional, and national records in all three disciplines of the sport.

Before we go any further, let me briefly explain the various disciplines. In the slalom event, the skier must complete a six-buoy course at a set boat speed of 34 mph for women and 36 mph for men. There are no form points in slalom skiing. The skier has only to enter a set of entrance gates, round the six buoys, and then exit the end gates.

This may sound easy, but with each successful run, the boat stops, and the official shortens the rope to make it more difficult. This shortening continues until the skier either misses or falls. At that point, their turn is over. In competition, most skiers will make four or five passes through the course before their turn comes to an end.

What is truly amazing is that during the skiers' final run, the rope is often several feet short of actually reaching the buoy. To get around such an impossible obstacle, the skier must be in perfect rhythm of leaning through the boat's wakes and changing the ski's direction prior to the buoy.

Although slalom skiing is where I achieved the most success, the trick event was by far my favorite. Trick skiing can be described as gymnastics on water. In this discipline, the skier is given two twenty-second passes to perform as many tricks as possible without repeating a trick. One pass is generally executed with the rope in the skier's hand, while the other pass is completed with the rope attached to the skier's foot. Judges determine whether the tricks are executed properly. If they are, they are assigned a point value. The winner is the skier with the most points.

Jumping was my least favorite event. To put it mildly, I was scared to death of jumping! It didn't help that my father habitually arrived at the starting dock prior to my turn with this message: "Be careful, baby. There are no heroes in this event. You respect that jump ramp...it can kill you!"

Thanks, Dad! Just what I needed to hear.

I can remember praying all the way down the lake as I prepared for my first jump, "Dear Lord, please help me not to die."

As soon as I landed on my feet, I'd breathe a sigh of relief, "Thank you, God!" Then I'd start the prayer process all over again for the next two attempts at the ramp. There's a reason they call each jump an *attempt*. On more than one occasion, I was carried off on a stretcher, straight to the hospital.

Despite the challenges and occasional injuries, however, I loved mastering new skills, twisting and turning on top of the water. In 1983, at the age of thirteen, I received an exclusive invitation to showcase my trick-skiing skills at the prestigious US Masters Water Ski and Wakeboard Tournament held annually at Callaway Gardens in Pine Mountain, Georgia. It was there that I entered my first international competition, competing against the top adult athletes in the world.

So much of the experience is ever so fresh in my memory...my first Master's jacket, hearing the National Anthem echo across the lake, standing on the dock looking into my mother's reassuring eyes as she gave me last-minute instructions, and hearing the screams of thousands of spectators as they cheered me on into the trick course. I'll also never forget hearing my father's distinct southern voice as he yelled, "You can do it, baby!" at the top of his lungs as the boat pulled away from the dock.

I loved every minute of it! Well, almost every minute—right up until I fell flat on my face in the middle of my first trick pass. The crowd's "Oh!" in perfect unison as I hit the water still rings loudly in my mind.

I still remember being under the water in total shock. How could this have happened? What did I do wrong? Did I hit a wave? Who put a banana peel in the middle of the lake?

Eventually my little lungs told my confused mind it was time to surface, and when I did, I had a choice to make. Should I swim to shore and quit or grab hold of the rope, tell the boat to "hit it," and give everything I had on my second run? I chose the latter.

It would be two years before I had the privilege of saying "hit it!" again at the US Masters. As I waited for my second invitation to compete, I continued to press on, holding tightly to hope. I knew that if I continued to work hard, the invitation would eventually come. And it did.

In 1985, at the age of fifteen, I was given a second chance. This time I didn't fall. Instead, I made my way to the end of both trick runs and came home the US Master's Trick Champion. And I did it again in 1986.

I can only wonder how different my life would have been had I refused to say "hit it!" after my fall at my first Masters. What if I had given up? What if I had allowed my fear, disappointment, frustration, and embarrassment to keep me from being willing to try again?

I can tell you what wouldn't have happened. I would have never been a two-time US Masters Trick Champion, six-time US Masters slalom champion, four-time US Open Champion, Pan Am Games Champion, World Champion, and world record holder for eighteen years. As an athlete, saying "hit it!" over and over again was without a doubt the best decision I ever made!

Yet I have to admit that saying "hit it!" wasn't always as easy as it was in the early days. As I excelled in the sport, many challenges emerged that often opposed my desire to continue. One of the biggest challenges was the constant physical pain I experienced due to a congenital hip deformity and spinal issues. There were also inconveniences such as unfair judgment calls, difficult conditions, tough competitors, and the constant pressure of staying on top. As you'll soon learn, my mind was often embroiled in one big wrestling match of powerful, anxious emotions that stole much of my joy. So many times I felt like yelling "I quit it!" rather than "hit it!"

But I didn't. In the end, no matter how many negative emotions attached themselves to those two little words, no matter how much I wanted to climb into the boat for the very last time, something (or I should say "Someone") was always right beside me in the water, giving me the strength to continue on. Somehow I found the courage to face my fears and overcome my frustrations. Why? Because I knew victory would only come if I refused to allow fear, anger, frustration, or guilt to keep me off the water. And more than anything, I wanted victory. I wanted to be the best I could be.

SOMETHING TO THINK ABOUT

As an athlete, wife, mother, and ministry leader, I've learned that the concept of "hit it" holds true in every aspect of life. Victory only comes when we are willing to get off the dock—that place of comfort—and say "Hit it!" despite our feelings, pain, or circumstances. Making the decision to give that command isn't always easy. I don't care who you are or what you do, every day will present its own set of challenges—challenges that can overwhelm us with emotions, making it difficult to even imagine ourselves taking the first step out onto the water. Sometimes we may even be tempted to say "I quit it!" in life.

Yet if we can come to a place where we are willing to say "hit it!" above all the emotions that flood our minds and above all the physical pain that ravages our bodies, victory will come. Just like in skiing, it may not come easily or quickly. In fact, it may even bring some pain. But if we persevere and refuse to give up, if we continue to say "hit it!" over and over again, we will move forward to our destiny.

My experience at Robin Lake as a thirteen-year-old girl taught me a valuable life lesson: it's not the disappointments in life that prevent success; rather, it's what we choose to do after the disappointment that determines our level of victory.

So often when people experience a failure or encounter an obstacle, they grow discouraged and quit. If only they would get fired up rather than fizzled out!

Champions fall. Champions fail. It's a fact in sports and in life. I've been described as one of the winningest female slalom skiers of all times—yet I can tell you with all certainty that I lost more competitions than I won. As long as you are willing to learn from your mistakes and press on, victory can still be yours.

Remember, it's not your disappointments and failures that prevent success. It's whether or not you choose to say "Hit it!" time and time again. The choice is up to you—will you swim to shore or keep on keeping on? Take it from me, victory could be only one "hit it" away!

CHAPTER 2

THE TEAM

*Two people are better off than one, for they can help each
other succeed. If one person falls, the other can reach out and
help. But someone who falls alone is in real trouble.*
ECCLESIASTES 4:9–10

Although water-skiing is an individual sport, it took a team to take me to
the top. In the early years of my career, my team consisted of my father,
mother, brother, and a group of close family and friends who traveled this
journey with us. In the latter part of my career, the responsibility of my
training shifted to my husband Tim, as he became my primary coach
and driver. Every member of my team brought much to the game—some
helped me mentally and emotionally, while others pushed me physically.
All of them provided exactly what I needed at every stage of my develop-
ment as a person and an athlete.

My dad was the innovator and the motivator. He would invent incredible ways to keep me moving forward, both on and off the water. Since we
lived in North Carolina, there were several months of the year where the
weather would prevent me from training. To keep me motivated during the
off-season, Daddy would invent creative ways to help build my balance and
confidence. He'd pull me across the grass on handmade saucers or have
me practice my tricks on the trampoline as I held onto a water-ski handle
attached to a pulley system.

On the water, Daddy was continually coming up with ways to get
me to try new things. He would create games that kept skiing fun while

challenging me to new levels. I vividly remember him standing on the motor box with his bullhorn, yelling, "Pull!" as I sliced through the wakes on my slalom ski. After crossing the second wake, he would then yell, "Turn!" as I approached the buoy. This continued throughout the entire course. These calls taught me the rhythm and technique I would need to be a successful slalom skier.

Daddy's bullhorn was indeed an effective tool in offering great instruction, but his bribery techniques were way more fun! Always a wheeler and dealer, he would make deals with me, saying things like, "Kristi, if you can do ten wake-backs in a row without falling, I'll buy you a baton!" I received the baton, although I didn't learn to twirl very well.

Daddy often used bribery as a way to motivate me, but I truly did love the sport. I loved the challenge, and I loved accomplishing what had been impossible the day before. Don't tell him, but I would have done it without the cash and toys.

While my father offered creativity and vision, my mother offered stability and comfort. She was my daily coach and my best friend. She was the one who spent hours upon hours on the water with me during the spring, summer, and fall months.

Every day during the training season, she would pick me up from school with boat in tow and an afternoon snack waiting for me on the car seat. During our nearly hour-long drive to the river, she would help me with my homework.

When we'd arrive at the marina, my mom would whip the boat into the water, and off we'd go. She was quite the multitasker. You should have seen her getting the boat up to speed and making sure the path was clear so that she could jump into the other seat and step into coaching mode. Since I was often doing tricks with the rope tied to my foot, my mother not only had to act as boat driver and coach, she had to take on the role of rope-release person as well. If I fell, her responsibility was to pull a cord that would release my ski rope from the pylon so that my leg didn't get injured. After a fall, Mom would jump back into the driver's seat, whirl the boat around, pick me up, give me some instruction, and take off again.

My mom also rode in the boat with me during trick events at tournaments. Somehow, she knew exactly what to say to me right before I entered the water. Her calm spirit brought a calmness to my own spirit.

Now that I am a mother, I am amazed at the sacrifice my mother made for me. She gave up her life for me and made it possible for me to be a champion. The only way I know how to repay her is to do the same thing for my children.

I know my mom was relieved when my brother came of age to drive the boat. If you consider five years old "of age." Just as God had put a passion in me to ski, He had put a passion in my brother Michael, to drive. He loved anything with a wheel and a motor. We have videos of my brother driving the boat while I, in true older sister mode, yell at him to maintain the boat speed. One of my favorite videos is of Michael grinning a huge snaggle-toothed smile at the camera proclaiming the obvious, "I don't get *no* respect!"

Our training situation presented many challenges. The Pamlico River was quite a distance away from our home; therefore, we spent a lot of time on the road and often returned home late at night. It was also a large body of brackish (partly salt) water. Skiing on salt water is very different from skiing on freshwater, due to the buoyancy of the water. Because tournaments were held in small freshwater lakes, it was difficult to effectively prepare for competitions.

There were also many distractions in the form of wind and waves and other boaters. To find privacy, we would take our inboard boat into shallow creeks where outboard boaters couldn't go and the waters were protected from the wind. No one interrupted our training there, except for occasional critters like jellyfish and snakes. One day my dad quickly snatched me out of the water and into the boat, ski and all, as a water moccasin aggressively swam right where I had been. From that day forward, someone was invariably on snake patrol.

Being on the river all day was often exhausting. Since we trained in back creeks, we were quite a distance from our river cottage and unable to head to the house for breaks. This was troublesome when storms would arise. When the wind and rain would begin to blow, we would have to take cover under the nearest bridge. This seemed like a good idea until one day when lightning traveled through the bridge and slammed my mom onto the motor box.

We spent many years on the Pamlico River, all the while creating incredible memories that I will forever cherish. But as my talents grew, the need for a private, freshwater training site emerged. If I was going to reach the top of the sport, I needed a place to practice without the interruptions of other boaters and the irritatingly painful stings of the summer jellyfish.

To meet this need, my father and mother decided it was time to build our own lake. It wasn't long before they found a large piece of property seven miles from our home in Greenville, North Carolina. I remember waiting in the back of our family car with my brother while my parents met with surrounding neighbors inside the landowner's home about their plan to dig a lake. The idea of digging a private lake wasn't a common one, and many people had concerns. Over time and with a lot of work, my father convinced the naysayers—even the bank—that his idea was sound.

As an eleven-year-old child, I really didn't understand the magnitude of my parents' undertaking. Didn't everyone dig their own lake? God had put quite a vision in my parent's heart, a vision that transformed a tract of farmland into one of the most beautiful places in the world. Little did we know how God would use Lake Kristi to touch thousands of lives in the coming years.

From the moment the lake filled up in 1982 until 1988 when I graduated from high school, my friend Jackie and I trained together on the waters of Lake Kristi with my mom as the primary coach. Long gone were the days of shooting imaginary witches out of the sky from the back of the boat. Now we had an incredible private place to train and a cabin to rest in between sets. It was an amazing setup, and both of our rankings quickly began to climb to a world level.

SOMETHING TO THINK ABOUT

Success cannot be achieved alone. There is no such thing as an individual sport or activity. Without fail, someone is hard at work behind the scenes helping you move forward in your dreams, and that someone always deserves a thank-you.

How thankful I am for the many people God placed in my life to help me accomplish my dreams. People like my family, personal sponsors, and friends, who assumed the roles of boat driver, coach, financial supporters, equipment providers, and cheerleaders. As well as the tournament organizers, corporate sponsors, and officials who provided a place for me to showcase my talents and compete. And finally, the many incredible, world-class competitors and training partners who constantly pushed my skills to new limits. Without them, I would have never reached my highest potential. To all of the above, I say thank-you.

Who has helped you to accomplish the desires of your heart? Have you told them how much you appreciate the sacrifices they have made and the support they have given? Why not take the time right now to give them a much deserved and, perhaps, long overdue thank-you?

CHAPTER 3

PARALLEL JOURNEY

*Direct your children onto the right path, and
when they are older, they will not leave it.*
PROVERBS 22:6

I wasn't the only person in our family who was making waves in the water-ski world. My father was making a pretty large wake of his own. About the same time I took off on water skis, my father began selling them. As I was twisting and turning my way to victory, my dad was wheeling and dealing on the shoreline.

When we began entering water-ski competitions in 1975, Daddy soon realized that having proper equipment was incredibly important. Skiers who want to improve their skills need the latest and greatest equipment to go along with their hard work and dedication. But obtaining new equipment in a timely fashion wasn't an easy task, as my father would soon discover.

In his quest to purchase skis, my dad began to call the water-ski manufacturers directly. With a little convincing, they agreed to send skis straight to our home. Daddy would then bring his new toys to the ski tournaments and share them with his ski buddies. I can still remember several men in bathing suits lined up at the trunk of our car, examining these priceless, manly treasures!

Before long, we had a store operating out of the back of our car as Daddy sold the new equipment to his competition. Pretty nice guy, huh? As interest in water skis grew, he decided to order larger quantities of items and sell them through mail order. All he needed now was a place to start his water-sports business. How about right dab in the middle of our family's supermarket? I can only imagine my grandfather's reaction when my father shared his vision of selling water skis next to the freshest meats in town!

I can still picture those beautiful water skis lined up on the wall behind the meat counter. Our first catalog had a slogan like none other: *Overton's...Competitive Skis at Supermarket Prices!* It wasn't long before my mom found herself in the back of the grocery store answering phone calls and taking orders.

An exciting thing to do as a child was to go with my parents to our store after hours. After hours meant two things: I was able to ride the pallet jack around the store (it was the original Razor™ skateboard!) and also make a selection of something yummy from the candy shelf.

One evening, I learned a great life lesson that led to an unforgettable experience. Instead of going to the candy aisle, I went to the medicine aisle and picked up what I thought was aspirin gum. I wanted to get around the no-chewing-gum rule at school, and this was the only acceptable way to do it. Although I had my parents' permission to get the gum, I sure wish I had let them read the label as I picked up laxative gum instead of aspirin gum. I can tell you from experience, they are not the same thing! The next day proved to be a L-O-N-G one as I spent hours in the school bathroom. One thing was for sure, none of my friends ever wanted to borrow gum from me again.

Eventually, the back of the grocery store had more skis than canned goods, so my parents decided it was time to expand. They built a showroom and warehouse next to the grocery store, complete with a call center and loading dock. Now my brother and I had even more space to ride the pallet jack and limitless areas to play hide and seek.

By the grace of God, Overton's grew into the world's largest watersports dealer. If you have ever owned a boat, you've probably received our magazine. In 2003, with the joy of running the business overshadowed by the stress of the economy, my parents decided to sell the company. Ironically, the very same day my father signed the official closing papers to sell Overton's was also the last time I skied publicly prior to my retirement in 2005. Pretty amazing that our careers began and ended at the exact same time.

As you can see, my dad was a visionary. Whether selling water skis or coaching his daughter, he was constantly thinking of new ways to keep our family moving forward to victory. He had big ideas backed by a huge heart that led him to take courageous steps of faith.

With the vision and dreams God placed within my father and the faithful support my mother gave him, many lives have been touched through the success of our family business, including my own. I learned so much from them both, by their words and most importantly by the way they lived and continue to live their lives. I am so thankful for their life examples. They have unfailingly been the same people behind closed doors as they are out in the open...people of love and faith.

From my father, I learned to be courageous and to step out into new territory—even if it meant very few were coming along. My father had to fight many external voices throughout his life that spoke against his ideas and ability to succeed. Thankfully, he made the decision to lay those voices aside and follow his heart instead. The result was a life journey that few people ever experience.

As he followed his heart and took incredible steps of faith, God's blessings began to pour into our lives. As God blessed my family, I learned the importance of being willing to pass our blessings on to others. I know without a doubt that my parents are blessed because they have continually been a blessing to others. They have given away more than they have ever kept for themselves.

Many people work hard to accumulate things and to achieve success, but when they get them, they hold on to them with clenched fists, as tightly as they can. Not Daddy. Both his heart and his hands have remained open, always giving to others, regularly sharing every success with those in his path, whether or not they deserve or appreciate it. I have witnessed first-hand how this willingness to give has allowed God the opportunity to flow His blessings through my dad and into the lives of others. He has truly been a vessel God has used to touch many lives.

Countless people have told me how my dad has helped them chase their dreams and move forward in life. And if animals could speak, they would tell the world how he has given them a chance at life. Our property at Lake Kristi is full of goats, cats, dogs, and horses who needed a place to live and recover from sickness and abuse.

I'm so thankful for the incredible character my father exhibited in his daily life. But I'm most grateful for his example of faith. The most beautiful sight I remember as a child was my father kneeling beside his bed in his red-checkered boxer shorts as he said his evening prayers. This is something he has continually done, every day of his life. Recently as an adult, I had the opportunity to share a hotel room with my parents. Words cannot express the joy I experienced when I looked over my shoulder to tell Daddy good night, only to find him kneeling between the hotel bed and wall… red-checkered boxers and all. I'm hoping they're not the same pair!

My mother has impacted my life just as much as my father. She too has a generous heart, but even more so, she has a servant's heart. Without hesitation, my mom puts other people's needs before her own. In doing so, she has taught me to love as Christ loves…unselfishly and unconditionally. She consistently laid her life down, her own dreams and desires, for the sake of others, especially her family's.

As my father and I chased our passions in the world of water sports, my mother was the one behind the scenes making it all possible. She was the one pulling me up and down the lake; she was the one keeping my father organized and on time for his many commitments; and she was the one helping my brother with homework and making sure he was achieving his dreams as well. If she ever minded, I'll never know. She isn't one to complain. To this very day, she has served others with joy and complete satisfaction. I am amazed at her stable, humble, and peaceful spirit. I believe it is a reflection of her spirit's contentment in Christ.

SOMETHING TO THINK ABOUT

Whether we see them or not, eyes are always watching. Therefore, it is vitally important to be people of character at all times, especially if we claim to be a Christian. My parents, especially my dad, constantly reminded me of this truth. He wanted to ensure that I reflected a Christlike attitude at all times—in victory and in defeat. To both him and my mom, this was more important than coming home with the gold.

After a disappointing run in competition, when all I wanted to do was scream and yell and chuck my ski across the water, I could always count on Dad to say, "Pull yourself together, baby. People are watching you." He could see what I couldn't—hundreds of pairs of eyes, some belonging to little children patiently waiting for an autograph, just waiting to see how I handled myself. I'm thankful for those reminders, as they kept me from acting foolishly and tainting my reputation.

I'll never fully know how maintaining my composure and integrity both on and off the water impacted others. Recently, however, I got a glimpse when a former boat judge shared how my turning down an opportunity for a reride in the US Open Championship, an event that had occurred over a decade prior, had affected him.

At that event, the officials in the boat had offered me a reride—a chance to try again—because they assumed that ducks in the course had caused me to fall early. But I knew the ducks hadn't been the culprit, and I turned down the chance to try again. Unknowingly, that simple action left an impression in the heart of this man that opened a door for my future words and actions in ministry to be well received.

You know, it's ironic. My parents often taught me the importance of maintaining character and integrity in the presence of others, but I wonder if they knew how closely I was watching them. Undoubtedly, the greatest influence my parents had on my life didn't come from the words they spoke, the things they bought me, or the opportunities they provided;

rather, it was the silent language of their daily actions. Their lives spoke volumes and set an example that showed me how to live and how to love.

Whether as an athlete or a parent, in the workplace or in ministry, it is ever so important to live a life above reproach. We never know when people are watching and how the language of our actions is speaking to hearts. What message are your life actions sending to those around you?

CHAPTER 4

HEADING SOUTH

For everything there is a season,
a time for every activity under heaven.
ECCLESIASTES 3:1

In 1988, I faced the tough decision of where to attend college. Part of me wanted to stay home. I loved North Carolina. Once you get that tar on your heels, it's hard to get it off. I also treasured being with my family and friends. I struggled leaving my family and my private training site, Lake Kristi. My parents had sacrificed so much financially, physically, and emotionally to build such an amazing place for me. How could I leave?

Yet in the depths of my heart, I knew that if I wanted to continue to have a successful professional career on the water, I needed to head south. I had been offered a full scholarship at the University of Central Florida in Orlando. Living in Florida would provide me with the opportunity to ski year-round, as well as train with top athletes on a daily basis.

Furthermore, I really needed a change to motivate me on the water. By this time, I was growing a bit stagnant in my performance, and my love for the sport was dwindling. Anger and frustration were beginning to replace the joy I had once experienced as a skier.

For months, I struggled with my decision—stay home or move south? It's all I could think about. I was so afraid that making one decision over the other would negatively impact the course of my life. More than anything, I wanted to make the right decision for my future.

As I think back, this was the first time in my life that I actually realized my need for God's wisdom. Until then, I had simply followed the decisions and directions of my parents. The decision of where I would attend college, however, was being left up to me.

One day as I drove down the road, I decided it was time to quit worrying and simply ask God to help me. I remembered that Philippians 4:6–7 says,

> Don't worry about anything; instead, pray about everything. Tell God what you need, and thank Him for all He has done. Then you will experience God's peace which exceeds anything we can understand. His peace will guard your hearts and minds as you live in Christ Jesus.

So I began to pray, "God, I need to know where I should go to college. I want Your wisdom and I need Your help."

It was a simple prayer but one backed by faith. I knew that only God knew my future and what would be best for my life.

Now, I don't know if you'll believe what happened next was truly a sign from God or not, but within seconds of those words coming out of my mouth, right there on that country road in North Carolina, a car with a Florida license plate sped past me and pulled right in front of my car.

A sign from above? Maybe not for some, but for me, that small green, orange, and white license plate settled the issue. I immediately felt peace in my spirit and soon sent in my acceptance letter to the University of Central Florida.

I have to smile as I think back to this time. Throughout the course of my Christian walk, God hasn't sent a lot of literal signs like that license plate my way. More often than not when I have asked for direction, I hear very little, if anything at all. That still, small voice the Bible refers to is just that—still and small. It's often hard to hear over the noise of the world and the noise of my emotions.

Yet at every stage of my life, when I have quieted my spirit and asked God to direct my footsteps, He has been faithful to show me the way to go. He's met me at every stage of my faith walk and given me exactly what I needed to move forward.

At eighteen, as a young girl with little knowledge of the Word and small faith, He gave me a bold, in-my-face license plate, just like He gave Moses a burning bush in the wilderness. It got my attention, and the direction couldn't be missed. But as I mentioned above, experiences like that have been rare.

The primary way God leads me in my decisions is through His Word, the Bible. As I have searched the scriptures, I've found direction for every issue of life. His Word has taught me how to interact with people, how to think, how to give, and how to act and react. It has shown me how to be a good steward of my finances and of other things, like the ministries and children that He has entrusted to me.

When I have faced decisions not specifically addressed in the Bible, God uses His Spirit to lead me and confirm the direction through circumstances and people. On more than one occasion, He has placed incredible desires in my heart, desires that rise from deep within my spirit and nudge me in one direction or another. I'll be giving you lots of examples in the upcoming chapters.

As I look back over my life, I am amazed. Whenever I have acknowledged my need for His wisdom and desired His will above my own, He has never failed to direct my footsteps. Yet, even after decades of seeking God and knowing there's a solid track record of faithfulness on His part, I still often struggle with making decisions, fearing that I am going to make a decision that will somehow screw up "the plan." You know…God's plan for my life.

I have often sat, paralyzed with fear, crying out to God, "Help me, Lord. I don't want to mess up!" One particular day, as I entered this familiar mental wrestling match about not messing up, I felt the Holy Spirit leading me to the first chapter of James. Verses five through eight caught my attention.

> If you need wisdom, ask our generous God, and He will give it to you. He will not rebuke you for asking. But when you ask Him, be sure that your faith is in God alone. Do not waver, for a person with divided loyalty is as unsettled as a wave of the sea that is blown and tossed by the wind. Such people should not expect to receive anything from the Lord. Their loyalty is divided between God and the world, and they are unstable in everything they do.

This passage hit me right between the eyeballs as I realized that, although I was asking God for wisdom and desiring His will for my life, I wasn't trusting His ability to lead me. I wasn't trusting His promise to give me wisdom to make the right decision. As a result, I was living in a world of doubt and instability.

Unstable is a perfect description of how I have often felt emotionally, mentally, spiritually, and physically. Doubt has had a tendency to keep me sidelined or cause me to run around in circles when I should be moving forward in confidence that God is not going to let me go astray.

Slowly but surely, I've been learning to lay aside my doubt and simply trust that as I seek God, He will be at work behind the scenes, directing my footsteps and orchestrating my life according to His will. I believe that as followers of Christ, God knows our hearts. He knows whether our hearts desire to follow His will or our own. As long as our hearts desire Him, God will gently move us forward; and if we need correction, He'll gently bring that, too. He did it for me as a young girl praying over her future, and He's faithfully led me as a wife, mother, and ministry leader. I know that He will do it for you, too!

Okay, it's time to get back to the story...

In August 1988, my mom and I packed up a U-haul and headed to my new apartment in Orlando. I can still vividly picture my father's tear-stained face in the rearview mirror as his little girl drove away.

Within months, I knew that my decision to move south was the right one. Not since I was a young girl had I enjoyed skiing this much. It was fun again. I was learning something new every time I went out on the water, and I was enjoying spending time with top male athletes who continually pushed me.

After a winter of training with these guys, I won my first professional slalom event at the age of nineteen. This win was exactly the spark I needed to rekindle my interest in the sport, a flame that burned for another fifteen years and brought me to the top of the podium many times.

During my college years, I spent a lot of time on the water with incredible athletes who poured their knowledge into me. Not only was I receiving top-notch instruction from legends, but I was also receiving a mental picture of what I was supposed to do. As a visual learner, this helped tremendously.

I also improved in my skill because of pride. I didn't want to be known as the "girl" on the lake, so I pushed myself to keep up with the guys. Trust me, they didn't cut me any slack! I quickly found myself skiing at a much higher level mentally and physically.

Time on the water got really exciting one day when one of my training partners, Kyle Tate, decided we should relocate to a different lake in Orlando. Seems he had met this guy named Tim Johnson, a free safety on the UCF football team, who had agreed to let us keep our ski team's boat at his lake home. At first, I really didn't want to leave my current location. I was performing well and enjoyed training with many incredible athletes who had helped me tremendously in my career.

Kyle, however, was persistent in persuading me to train at Tim's lake. He finally broke through my arguments with this statement, "Kristi, I have met the guy you're going to marry!" It's no surprise that Kyle is now a successful attorney; he's relentless!

As I look back, I can see God's invisible hand at work. Not only did my performance on the water continue to improve, but God did, indeed, also bless me with an incredible husband in Tim and a lifelong friendship with Kyle and his family. When asked how Tim and I met, I tell people that I used Tim for his lake, and he used me for my boat! It was a match made in heaven.

SOMETHING TO THINK ABOUT

Often times, people are afraid of change. They fear failing in their new environment, failing in their attempt at a new endeavor, or perhaps, disappointing someone in the process. Some people may even fear the challenges that change will inevitably bring.

The reality, however, is that change is necessary for growth. Only by pushing yourself out of your comfort zone, being willing to put yourself out there, and laying aside your emotions can you move toward victory.

Will it always be easy? No. Will you make mistakes and perhaps disappoint someone by your choice to make a change? Yes. Will it be a bit overwhelming and scary at times? Yes. Anything unfamiliar can be. Regardless of all of this, however, you must choose to make a move if God is leading you forward.

Because I made a decision to step out of my comfort zone and move to Florida, I grew in my abilities, mental toughness, and in my relationships both with people and God. I stepped into a whole new realm of victory spiritually and as a professional athlete, accumulating not only professional slalom titles but also world record performances.

We must realize that there is a real danger in making the choice to stay put out of fear or complacency. It's the danger of becoming stagnant...and with stagnation comes discontentment, lack of growth, and lack of joy.

So how about it? Have you been hanging back in your comfort zone? Perhaps it's time to step out into the deep with God. Don't worry, He's got your back!

CHAPTER 5

OPPOSITE ENDS OF
THE SPECTRUM

*Why worry about a speck in your friend's
eye when you have a log in your own?*
MATTHEW 7:3

I remember perfectly my first day of training at Tim's lake in the spring of 1990. As Kyle and I drove into Tim's driveway, Tim was climbing out of his blue Toyota truck to check his mailbox. I have to admit, I enjoyed watching this incredibly athletic and handsome football player walk to and from his car. I smiled as I realized he was the same guy who had been catching my attention around campus.

It didn't take long for Tim to start riding in the boat while Kyle and I trained. Each morning, he would walk down to the boat with a large glass bowl full of cereal. As I made my way through the slalom course, Tim would munch away on his Lucky Charms. Suddenly, I didn't mind getting up early before school to train. I had a new incentive!

A few months after Tim and I met, it became obvious that we had a mutual affection for one another. I kept hoping he would ask me out, but he was a bit slow in that department. So, one day when we were out in the boat, I made my move. I challenged Tim with a friendly wager. I told him if he made a 360-degree turn across the wakes on his wakeboard, I would buy him dinner. He smiled and said, "Hit it!" He made the very next one he tried.

True to my word, I took Tim out to dinner and then waited for him to come knocking on my door for our next date. I had made the first move, something that is truly against the rules of a Southern girl, and I wasn't about to make the second. A couple of days later, the knock came.

From that day forward, we were inseparable, quickly becoming each other's best friend. Tim spent a lot of time in the boat with Kyle and me. His knowledge in the sport increased daily as he watched us train and listened to us coaching one another. Tim soaked in knowledge like a sponge—knowledge he would use to coach me for the next decade.

After dating for four years, during which time we both graduated from UCF with business degrees, Tim proposed to me in April of 1994. We knew we wanted to attend the University of Florida College of Law in the fall, so we decided on a summer wedding a mere three months away. People were a bit shocked at our brief engagement.

A few rumors circulated as to why we were getting married so fast. We weren't hiding any little secret, we simply wanted to get married before we entered law school. Thankfully, I had an incredibly organized mother who was able to take the bull by the horns and get everything done in such a short time.

On July 23, 1994 (the only summer weekend I had off from the professional ski tour), Tim and I made our vows before God in my hometown of Greenville, North Carolina. The ceremony was followed by a beautiful reception at Lake Kristi. After a two-day honeymoon at my parents' beach house in Wilmington, North Carolina, we returned to Lake Kristi to train for one day before heading to St. Louis for a professional competition. That weekend I celebrated my first professional slalom win as Kristi Overton Johnson.

Within a month of our marriage, Tim and I packed up a U-haul and headed from Orlando to our new home in Keystone Heights, Florida, to begin law school at the University of Florida. Keystone Heights is a small rural town about thirty minutes east of Gainesville. We chose this location because of its beautiful lakes, but we didn't plan to stay past the three years it would take us to graduate from law school.

For the next three years, Tim and I spent a lot of time together hitting the books and hitting the water. We got up very early in the morning to train before driving into Gainesville for our classes. Tim was willing to pull me anytime of the day, and he never complained unless I tried to make him ski with me. Tim isn't much of an early morning skier—in fact, he has two standing rules: no skiing before noon, and no skiing at all unless both the water and the air temperatures are above 70 degrees.

I enjoyed law school. I enjoyed the routine of training and studying. I also enjoyed being challenged mentally, emotionally, and physically. It may sound strange, but I have always thrived on having several things going on in my life at the same time. It keeps me from getting too focused on one activity, and it also keeps me from getting bored. It's just how I am wired.

I watched many people in law school become so focused on their studies that there was little room for anything else in their lives. Likewise, I witnessed many professional skiers get so wrapped up in their training and performance on the water that there was little joy in their lives. Having responsibilities on and off the water helped me stay balanced emotionally, although it was often tough physically. I studied hard, don't get me wrong; but when I got home from school, I laid aside the books and hit the water. Similarly, when I finished training, I returned back to the house, set my emotions aside, and got back to my studies.

As a young law student, I loved being married to Tim. We got along really well, on and off the water. This would have completely shocked our marketing professor from UCF! About two years into our courtship, Tim and I had taken a marketing class together that required us to complete a personality assessment. With the results in hand, the professor asked the class where Tim Johnson and Kristi Overton were sitting. Of course, we were sitting next to each other.

The teacher looked horrified and said, "You two better move across the room from each other. You have the most incompatible personality scores I've ever seen!"

Although the professor's prediction of incompatibility has been proven completely wrong, the results of the personality test were pretty accurate. Tim and I are vastly different. For example, he is quiet and rarely shares what's going on between his ears. I, on the other hand, have to work extra hard on keeping my mouth shut as I like to think out loud. Tim is happy with the status quo; I like change and am constantly pushing for improvement. Tim is at complete peace with himself; I've often found it difficult to feel quite good enough. Tim does what Tim wants to do, refusing to allow anyone to push him in a direction he doesn't want to go. I have habitually been concerned with what people think and usually put the desires and opinions of others ahead of my own. These are just a few of the many differences in our personalities.

Our professor was right—we are at opposite ends of the personality scale; but it is our differences that make our marriage so strong. Together, Tim and I make quite a team because we make up for one another's weaknesses. For example, Tim helps keep me in balance emotionally and physically. When I get going 100 mph in several different directions, he knows just what to say to bring me back to reality. He also keeps me grounded emotionally by his calm but confident nature. On the other hand, I push Tim out of his comfort zone and help him dream big. I also bring organization and productivity to the household.

Although different in personalities, we are still very much the same in core values and beliefs. We are both committed to growing in our relationship with God and with one another, and strengthening our family. We are also committed to living a healthy and active lifestyle.

Our love for one another and our commitment to God and family have motivated us to work through every difference. It hasn't always been easy. Like any marriage, we've had our challenges. Things like sickness, loss, setbacks, personal desires, financial stress, and disappointments have brought stress and presented opportunities for division.

I'm the first to admit that my strong type A personality presented a huge challenge early in our marriage. As an athlete, my determination to persevere until I reached my goal helped me to achieve great success on the water, but it wasn't necessarily a great trait for a relationship. To get what I wanted, I often pushed Tim in directions he didn't want to go. I wasn't usually successful, but I sure gave it my all.

I had my own ideas of what Tim should do for a living, how he should act and dress, and even how he should spend his time. I even went to law school in hopes that my decision to go would cause Tim to go. Surely I needed a successful lawyer as my husband. My plan worked...well, almost. We both went to the University of Florida College of Law, graduated, and passed the Florida Bar Exam. But neither one of us ever practiced law, not one single day. Tim became a residential contractor, and I went into ministry. So much for my plans, huh?

My strong personality also made for stressful moments when it came to making decisions for our household. To put it mildly, I didn't like someone involved in my decision-making processes. Since a teenager, I had been compensated to water-ski. I was used to being independent and making decisions, especially financial ones, on my own.

Fortunately for me, Tim has the wisdom of Solomon and the patience of Job. He also possesses a peace that passes all understanding. I've rarely seen Tim get anxious or upset. I have to admit, this lack of anxiety can drive me nuts! At first it seemed to me that he just didn't care about things as much as I did.

To help Tim change "for the better," I've often gone to the throne of God for a little help. Two instances pop into my mind. One time I asked God to help Tim be more concerned about the issues of life. I know that sounds crazy, but at that point in my life, I worried about everything. I couldn't understand why Tim didn't.

Upon my request, I was shocked to actually hear the following reply in the depths of my heart. "Tim is at perfect peace. I'm trying to get you to be more like him!" Talk about a reality check!

On another occasion, I asked God to help Tim become more spiritual. His relationship with the Lord was so different than mine. I couldn't understand why he didn't get up in the wee hours of the morning to study the Word of God with Bible commentaries and dictionaries in hand. I also didn't understand why he didn't have a desire to share his faith publicly in front of large crowds. Because of these and other differences, I judged Tim's spiritual condition—a dangerous thing to do.

Once again, God set me straight with His answer to my prayer, "Leave Tim alone. He and I are just fine."

Well, I am happy to say that with God's help over the years, I have mellowed quite a bit. I'm more patient, less anxious, and more at peace. I'm also less demanding and less judgmental. The turning point came the day I stopped pointing my finger at Tim, asking God to change him, and instead asked God to reveal to me what needed to be changed in my own life. As I allowed God to go to work, the peace and patience Tim had been experiencing began to be mine. Furthermore, the things I'd felt I had to fight so hard for, mostly material things, just didn't seem so important anymore.

It took me many years to learn to let Tim be Tim and if need be, to let God change Tim. It was a lesson worth learning. I am so thankful that Tim never became that person that I and sometimes others thought he should be. If he had, our lives would have been dramatically different. The only way our family is able to fulfill the calling God has placed on our lives is because each one of us is operating within the gifts He has given to us and being who He designed us to be.

SOMETHING TO THINK ABOUT

God created people differently. We all have unique gifts and personalities. We all have strengths and weaknesses. A problem arises when we believe our role is to change people or to fix them.

Through my marriage and other relationships, I've learned that only God can change a person's heart and their actions. When we start trying to change people, we get in the way of what God desires to do.

Our role isn't to change people to be who we think they should be. Rather, our role—and only role—is to love the Lord with all our heart, soul, strength, and mind, and to love the world to Him. People are transformed through our love and prayers, not our judgmental words and pressure. As we give people and situations to God, we will see God do what only He can do...change people from the inside out.

I've also learned that only God can bring true contentment into our lives. So often we try to change people in hopes that they will make us happy. People can't make us happy; only God can bring true joy.

Is there someone you have been trying to fix? Perhaps it's time to release them to the Lord and let Him do what only He can do.

CHAPTER 6

---◈◈◈---

HIT IT, GOD!

If you refuse to serve the Lord, then choose
today whom you will serve....
But as for me and my family, we will serve the Lord.
JOSHUA 24:15

For two decades, Tim and I resided in the rural town of Keystone Heights. Neither of us dreamed we would live there so long. God used this small, quaint town to help keep us focused on our faith and our relationship with one another. It was a wonderful fit for us and protected us from many outside pressures that perhaps would have distracted us from the good God had in store.

When we moved to Keystone Heights, there wasn't a lot there for a young married couple to do. Although we were busy with our studies and my training, we still longed for relationships and social interaction. We found both at our local church. It was there that we met wonderful people who loved us and treated us like family. While there, we also deepened in the most important relationship of all...our relationship with Jesus Christ.

Tim and I thought we had moved to Keystone Heights for the many beautiful lakes. We now know that God brought us there to fill us up with His Living Water, so we'd never thirst again. It was in this isolated place that we heard God's invitation to move out onto the waters with Him, and we accepted it.

For the first time in my life, I had a hunger for God. Before this time, I had attended church and read the Bible more out of duty, feeling as though it was expected of me. Now, I went to church and studied His Word because I wanted to. I had a true desire to know Him in a more intimate way.

As I look back over my life, I can see God's heart and His hand at work in so many ways, ever so gently guiding me along His path. As a child, He blessed me with a loving family who took me to church regularly and who lived a life of faith both publicly and at home. I was also blessed to have godly grandparents, aunts, uncles, and teachers who built on this foundation.

In Keystone Heights, God used our local church, pastor, and Sunday School teachers to further deepen our faith. He also used Christian television evangelists and Bible teachers. Through their teachings, God drew me into a deeper place with Him and began to open my spiritual eyes to new truths.

One key person in my faith journey was Mr. Ralph Meloon, one of the original founders of Correct Craft Boats, now known as Nautique. For decades, I had the privilege of representing this amazing Christian company as a contracted athlete. Mr. Ralph, now well into his nineties, has incessantly been a man of great faith who inspires many as he passionately shares his love for the Lord with anyone he meets. Since my teens, Mr. Ralph has served as an incredible accountability partner for me as he has constantly challenged me to share my faith through the platform of water-skiing.

"Kristi," Mr. Ralph would say, "we are soon heading over to France for the World Championships. I need you to give your testimony about your faith in Jesus Christ."

Invitations like these kept me on my spiritual toes. You see, although I was a believer in Jesus Christ, I wasn't faithfully following Him. My life choices didn't always line up with God's will for my life. Mr. Ralph's invitations to speak challenged me to ensure my life testimony matched my words. The last thing I wanted was for my life to be a stumbling block to keep someone else from knowing God.

Throughout my water-ski career, Mr. Ralph provided many opportunities for me to share my faith in countries such as Canada, Russia, France, and Singapore. How thankful I am that Mr. Ralph never quit calling. His calls helped me continue to seek Christ and to know Him more. How thankful I am, too, for his faithful and passionate walk with the Lord. He has encouraged me to stay strong until the day God calls me home.

Another gentleman who had a great impact in my spiritual life was Jerry Major. At the time, Jerry and his wife, Marilyn, were very involved with the summer camp program at Word of Life (WOL) Camp in Schroon Lake, New York.

Back in the mid 90s, Jerry, an avid water-skier, attended one of my professional competitions in Connecticut. After I competed, Jerry walked over to me and asked me for my autograph. He also asked if I would consider coming to speak to the youth at WOL. He looked a little surprised when I quickly replied, "Sure, I'd love to."

It wasn't long before I was heading to the camp's island in the middle of Schroon Lake. Although I had attended church my whole life, at that point in my faith, I really didn't understand what it meant to be a Christian. I believed in Jesus Christ with all my heart. I knew that out of God's great love for me, He had sent His Son, Jesus, to pay the price for my sin. Because of my faith in His sacrifice, according to the Word of God, my eternal salvation was secured (John 3:16).

But while I had asked Jesus to be my Savior, I had not made Him Lord of my life. It was on this isolated island that God, through the lives of the young campers and their staff, began to reveal to me the truth that Christianity is more than a mere belief in His existence. It is about an intimate relationship with Him through His Son Jesus Christ.

I remember the sting in my heart as I stood in front of approximately five hundred teenagers, telling them to live their lives for Christ. I didn't even have a clue what that meant! I stepped off that stage and made my way to my cabin, and there I fell down on my knees and cried out to God.

I asked Him to forgive me for being such a hypocrite. I also asked Him to give me what those teens had…a relationship.

I was tired of the mere routine of religion. Surely there was more to following Christ than going to church and standing up in front of people every now and then and telling them I am a believer. With a tender heart, I asked God for more. In that little cabin, in the middle of a stained floor, accompanied by a few crawling critters, I committed my life wholeheartedly to Him.

"Lord," I cried, "I want to know You in a real and personal way. Take my life, it's Yours."

In addition to this simple prayer, I also vowed to know God more each and every day of my life. As in my ski career, I committed to push myself spiritually. It has been this promise and commitment that has continually driven me deeper and deeper into His Word and caused me to consistently grow in my faith.

SOMETHING TO THINK ABOUT

So often people use the excuses of "I'm too young" or "I'm too old" to stay in their spiritual comfort zones. Because of their age, they don't think their words or actions will impact someone's life. Well, I am a living testimony that anyone, no matter their age, can radically change someone's life.

Those teenagers at Word of Life Camp impacted my life in a most profound way, and they didn't even had to say a word! Simply witnessing the power of Christ at work in their lives caused me to want what they possessed. I bet those campers would never have suspected that their lives could cause the guest speaker to rededicate her life to Christ. But they did.

Similarly, Mr. Ralph could have used the excuse of age and taken an earned seat in his rocking chair. He's in his nineties, for goodness' sake! But he hasn't. Rather, he continues to make the daily choice to go and tell the world the Good News of Jesus Christ. Had those teens or Mr. Ralph used age as an excuse, my life might have been very different.

People also allow fear to cause them to shrink back from following God's lead, perhaps to invite, encourage, or correct someone in love. Jerry could have easily thought of a number of excuses that would have prevented him from inviting me to visit Word of Life Camp. He could have concluded I'd be too busy, or perhaps wrongly reasoned that a professional skier wouldn't come to his camp.

Praise God, he didn't. And because of his boldness, I wholeheartedly committed my life to Christ.

My friend, don't ever let fear keep you from being bold for Christ. Don't allow excuses to get in the way of following God's lead. Your words and actions may be the nudge someone needs to take them to the next level spiritually...and to influence the world.

CHAPTER 7

CHOPPY WATERS

I have told you all this so that you may have peace in Me.
Here on earth you will have many trials and sorrows.
But take heart, because I have overcome the world.
JOHN 16:33

When I asked God to reveal Himself to me so that I could know Him more, I didn't really consider the circumstances I might have to go through to discover just how real and amazing He is. Now, don't get me wrong, I'm not suggesting that God, my loving Heavenly Father, hurled terrible circumstances in my path to teach me lessons. That would be like me deliberately causing my children pain to teach them something. I would never do that, and I don't think it is His habit either.

I can't deny, however, that God has allowed me to go through some tough and disappointing times. Yet, as I look back over my life, I am so thankful that He did. Through every trial, as I've turned to Him for wisdom, strength, and provision, He has revealed His faithfulness over and over again, and ultimately brought me into a deeper and more trusting relationship with Himself.

Until 1997, I had been fairly "circumstance" free. Of course, I had disappointments, aches, and pains like every athlete, but overall, I was healthy and happy. I was living what some would call a fairy tale life with an incredibly supportive family, a successful athletic career, financial security, and degrees from top universities. It was the fall of 1996, and I was coming off a series of world record performances, including my world record run that would last for fourteen years. I came into the winter months on an all-time high, eager to push myself to new limits and excited to finish my last year of law school.

In March of 1997, Tim and I made our way to Australia, where I kicked off the season with an exciting slalom win at the Moomba Masters in front of tens of thousands of people. Upon our return home, we decided it was time to start a family. We carefully planned the pregnancy so that I could compete at a majority of events in 1997 and have plenty of time to prepare for the 1998 tour season. By May, we were expecting our first child. We actually discovered I was pregnant on my last day of law school. As we shared the news at the US Masters, our family and friends joined in our excitement.

In June, however, something happened that rocked my world. Tim and I had temporarily moved to North Carolina for the summer so that I could focus on my training and help my parents prepare for the upcoming US Open Water Ski Championship that was scheduled to be held at Lake Kristi. This would be our family's second year hosting the event.

It may seem strange to some that I would continue to compete during my pregnancy, but it really wasn't uncommon for expectant women on the professional circuit to compete, sometimes well into their twentieth week. It was the only way we could keep ourselves from falling down the professional world-rankings list, a ranking system that determined an athlete's ability to compete in competitions the following year. My plan didn't last very long!

About ten weeks into my pregnancy, I began to have nagging stomach pain. Initially, I wasn't alarmed as I assumed the stress of studying for the Florida Bar, training intensely, and preparing to entertain the ski world at our home was shifting my nerves into high gear. Ever since I was a little girl, I had suffered from extreme stomach pain during competitions as the pressure to perform often got the best of me.

But two days prior to the preliminary round of the US Open, the pain in my stomach escalated to an intolerable point. I kept pushing, trying to put on a smile and entertain those I felt responsible to host, but eventually I couldn't take the pain any longer. I went to our lake cabin and laid down. It wasn't long before waves of nausea sent me to my knees. This cycle went on until the middle of the night when there was nothing left but green bile. Reasoning that something was terribly wrong, Tim called my parents and told them he was taking me to the hospital.

For over a day, the doctors failed to find a diagnosis for my symptoms. Fortunately, my pain level had subsided due to my new friend, morphine. I remember lying in the hospital bed, watching news from Lake Kristi flash across the television, wishing I could be at the lake. At one point, I even dragged my IV and morphine pump into the bathroom where I crouched down on the floor in a skiing position to see if I could possibly get up on a ski.

Throughout my whole life I had constantly pushed through physical pain—that's what athletes do. Surely I could push through this. Never before had I not been able to ski, and I didn't like it one bit, especially since the competition was being held at my lake in front of my hometown! I felt I needed to get to Lake Kristi and welcome my friends and fans to my lake. I also wanted to defend my title as the US Open Champ.

Fortunately, no matter how much I tried to convince Tim to take me to the lake, he wouldn't listen. It's a good thing, too, because a few hours later we discovered the source of my pain. Just when the hospital was about to discharge me, Tim noticed something strange about my belly button. It had grown to the size of a silver dollar. When he asked the doctor about it, he simply replied, "That's what happens to pregnant women."

My husband, looking a bit insulted, quickly responded, "She's only ten weeks pregnant. She isn't even showing yet!"

Within moments, I was rushed into surgery. Upon examination of my bowels, the doctors found several obstructions caused by scar tissue that had developed from my appendectomy, a surgery I had had six months prior. These thick, rubber-band like objects were constricting my intestines in various places. According to the doctors, I was minutes away from my intestines bursting, which could have easily led to a life-threatening infection for me and my unborn child.

After the surgery, I spent ten days in the hospital, munching on ice chips as I waited patiently for my bowels to start working again. Every day the doctor would come to my room with his team of interns and ask me questions that seemed a bit personal. You know, questions about whether I was having a successful bowel movement and/or passing gas. Gross, I know. It didn't take long for me to realize that a positive response to these questions was my ticket home. What's a girl to do but to start praying? That's right, I prayed for gas and poop. Praise God, He answered my prayer, and I was soon released.

My time during the hospital was trying in many ways. First of all, I was extremely concerned about the life of my child, as the doctors were having difficulty finding a heartbeat. With the incredible trauma we had both been through, there was much concern over whether my little one would make it. I was also facing physical pain that was very different from anything I had ever experienced as an athlete. This wasn't a backache or neck pain that I could simply push through. In this situation, I had no choice but to rest and wait for my body to heal.

The physical pain was nothing, however, compared to the emotional battle I faced. For the first time in my life, I couldn't be "Kristi, the skier." I watched helplessly from the sidelines as other skiers took my place on the podium, claimed my paycheck, and were featured in the magazines. I was quickly humbled as the world of water-skiing kept right on going without me as if I'd never existed.

I felt very confused and alone. Water-skiing had been my everything— my identity, my purpose, my worth, my financial security, and my happiness. In a word, it was my life, and now, in an instant, it was gone. I found myself pondering the question, "If I'm not 'Kristi the skier,' who am I?"

I wasn't sure, but there was one thing I did know: I wasn't ready for my ski career to be over just yet. As I waited for my bowels to heal and my son to be born (a seven-month period), a burning desire grew within me to get back on the water. There was so much more I wanted to accomplish in this sport. As soon as my doctor gave me medical clearance to ski after my C-section, I was right back on the water and in the gym, training harder than ever.

Ty, our beautiful newborn, simply came along for the ride. Tim and I referred to him as our "pack and go" baby. We just packed him up and went. If we were heading to the lake to train, Ty was right there too, safely secured in his car seat. The sound of the boat's engine would gently lull him fast asleep. If we were traveling to a competition, Ty came too.

At eleven weeks old, Ty was already earning frequent flyer miles and stamps in his passport as we made our way to Australia to compete in the exciting Moomba Masters. I had only been training for two weeks prior to the event, but I competed in this professional competition in order to accumulate much needed tour points. I was already behind on the world ranking list, as I had missed most of the 1997 season due to my pregnancy and surgeries.

Looking back, I should have stayed home rather than push my body so soon. I set a poor performance in Australia, which left a mark on my mental confidence that was harder to overcome than my physical weakness. At the time, however, my focused, determined, and competitive mind refused to consider any option other than taking my infant to the other side of the world so I could ski for a few minutes.

In 1998, I worked extremely hard to regain my position as the number-one ranked women's water-skier in the world, to no avail. No matter how hard I tried, the victories wouldn't come. Rediscovering my pre-surgery, pre-baby form on the water was harder than I could have ever imagined. My body was weak, and my mind was growing discouraged.

My disappointments on the water were soon joined by another disappointing medical blow off the water. In July of that year, just a week after I returned from a professional event in Russia, I found myself again doubled over in excruciating stomach pain. This time I didn't need to vomit up bowls of bile to know that I was experiencing another bowel obstruction. Without delay, the doctors navigated their way through my intestines, removing the rubber-band like tissues that were blocking my bowels.

Overnight, I found myself off the water and back at the starting dock of recovery. As I recovered physically, I began to question God spiritually. I wanted a reason. I wanted a "why" for what I was going through.

Was God punishing me? Was He trying to teach me a lesson? Was Satan attacking me? Did I not learn enough the first go-around that I was having to go through this again? Little did I know there would be many more bowel obstructions and other surgeries to follow.

I never really got clear answers to these questions. If God allowed these trials to strengthen my faith and reveal more about His character and my worth in Him, then mission accomplished. If on the other hand, these trials were sent by Satan to destroy my life and cause me harm, he failed, for God has used every trial for good in my life (Genesis 50:20).

I've often wondered if perhaps Satan knew how much skiing meant to me and hoped that by taking it away, he could cause me to lose hope or perhaps become bitter and pitiful. But I didn't. Instead, with every trial, I sought God more and more, looking to Him to be my strength and my purpose. As a result, I began to discover true intimacy with God and true identity in Him.

I was still hungry to compete, even after this surgery. This time around, however, my priorities had changed. With an appendectomy, emergency C-section, and two life-threatening bowel obstructions in eighteen months, I had begun to realize the preciousness of life and the temporariness of water-skiing. Instead of rushing out on the water as I had done previously,

I took the time to get physically strong and mentally prepared before I put myself back in competition.

This decision paid off. When I returned to competition in 1999, I was stronger than ever—mentally, physically, and spiritually. Over the next few years (1999–2001), I accumulated twenty-five professional slalom titles, despite a neck fusion in the fall of 2000. During this time, Tim and I and pack-and-go Ty traveled the globe, seeing the most beautiful sights and forming lifelong friendships with amazing people around the world. I'll treasure these experiences and friendships as long as I live.

Thinking back, I can say with all truthfulness that I'm thankful for every scar on my body. Each one presented me the opportunity to experience God's strength, presence, and provision in a deeper way. In Job 42:5, after Job had gone through some incredible trials—far greater than anything I have ever gone through—he said to the Lord, "I had only heard about You before, but now I have seen You with my own eyes."

Because Job had undergone such tremendous trials and looked to the Lord for strength and answers, he knew the Lord in a more intimate way; he knew Him by experience. I now know God by experience. And I will never be the same.

SOMETHING TO THINK ABOUT

As a water-skier, I spent much time searching for one thing—calm, peaceful water. I remember as a young girl dreaming that my parents would build a dome over our private lake. With a dome of protection, I'd be able to train in perfect conditions all year round. Never again would I have to face the trials of the wind, the rain, or the cold. Wouldn't that be something?

I have to laugh when I think about all the time I spent wishing and waiting for perfect conditions…as well as all the time I wasted complaining when I failed to experience them. But you know what? The turning point of my career came the day that I decided to quit fighting the elements and simply face them. Victory came when I quit complaining about the obstacles and instead, found a way to ski through them. Growth came when I quit sitting on the sidelines, courageously stepped out of my comfort zone, and allowed those conditions to stretch me.

Isn't it ironic that the very thing I desired on the water as a skier is the very thing people long for in life? Calm, still waters. We all prefer perfect conditions to rough water. I bet we'd all leap for joy if someone would just build a dome over our lives so we could be free from unpleasant, challenging circumstances and the interruptions of other people. I know I've often longed for the dome!

But you know what? Calm, uninterrupted waters aren't a reality in water sports or in life. Even Jesus promises that in this world, we will have trials and tribulations (John 16:33).

Sometimes the world just seems like one big ocean. But as I've faced each wave with Christ, I've found several things to be true. First of all, God doesn't guarantee a life free of obstacles and interruptions; rather, He promises a life of peace in the midst of them. I've also learned that, no matter how rough the water, there is no wave that is too big for God. Finally, I've learned that I'm never alone. Without fail, God is right there in the midst of even the choppiest of water preventing the waves from overtaking me (Isaiah 43:2). And He's there with you, too.

Is there some obstacle you are wishing God would remove? It may just be the very thing that brings you closer to Him.

CHAPTER 8

SKIING FOR A DIFFERENT PURPOSE

So whether you eat or drink, or whatever
you do, do it all for the glory of God.
1 CORINTHIANS 10:31

After I made my commitment to know God more at Word Of Life Camp, and after the physical trials that soon followed, a passion began to develop in my heart to truly live for Christ. No longer did I want mere religion, I wanted a relationship with Him, and I wanted to be used by Him. Through my surgery experiences, I quickly learned that the things of this world and my plans could vanish in an instant. I wanted my life, even my skiing, to have eternal value.

While competing on tour during the early 2000s, God began to show me ways that He could use the very thing I loved—water-skiing—and the international platform that He had given me in that sport to bring people to a personal relationship with Him. He also began to stretch my faith and show me incredible spiritual things, especially about Himself.

The first thing He led me to do was partner with other Christian athletes to hold church services at various professional water-sports events around the world. Although these were simple gatherings, often under a hospitality tent or in a small hotel room, God began to move. As water-sports athletes, judges, drivers, sponsors, tour organizers, and fans came together to worship God, lives began to change, hearts were encouraged, bonds were created, and hope was found.

As I experienced God's presence in such a powerful way at these services, I began to realize many important truths. First of all, I realized that God isn't too concerned with where His people gather to worship or how we dress; rather, He's concerned with our hearts. Even though we were on the side of a lake, under a tent, and dressed in T-shirts and shorts, God was still there. As we praised Him and gave testimony to what He had done in our lives, He moved in our midst. I really don't think our attire and lack of formality bothered Him one bit. In fact, I believe He was very pleased because He saw the intentions of our hearts...we were unified children of the King, coming together to praise His name.

Secondly, I realized God isn't concerned with our choice of denomination, as long as Jesus Christ is the center of it. Until this point, I had only been exposed to one Christian denomination and was basically under the impression that any other denomination was wrong or off base in some way. Yet as I worshipped with people from many other denominations, I couldn't deny the love and devotion they had for God. It was real, and their faith was strong. I learned so much as we all came together, united in the precious name of Jesus.

I have come to believe that more times than not, way too much emphasis is placed on outward appearance, on style and place of worship, and on following traditions when all God is truly concerned with is the heart of a man. He simply desires people to unite in their Christ-centered faith and love Him and each other with a pure heart.

The church services began to grow, and God ever so gently began to tug at my heart, inviting me to step out even deeper with Him. To this point, stepping out for Christ had been pretty easy and fun. I enjoyed partnering with other athletes to organize the services. I was developing lifelong friendships and being encouraged in my faith. I also loved speaking publicly about the things of God, especially to people who had a heart to listen. But I soon sensed God wanting me to do more than just come together with other believers. He wanted me to share His love and truth with nonbelievers, especially my peers, in a more bold way.

Although most people on tour knew I was a Christian, I had shied away from personally sharing with anyone about the love of God and His plan for salvation. Oh, I had been faithful to give Him the praise for my victories, whether it was on ESPN, in the newspapers, magazines, or on the microphone. I knew that my gifts and abilities had been given to me by God, and I wanted to make sure He was given the glory He deserved.

Sadly though, despite my faithfulness to give God glory for my accomplishments, I had failed to share how someone could truly know the One to whom I gave thanks. Why? Because I was afraid of what would happen if I did. Perhaps they would laugh, poke fun, or worse, be offended and reject me. My whole life I had had one goal...to be liked by everyone. Stepping out and saying something that many people would possibly disagree with or think was foolish would put me in a position to be ridiculed and outcast. It was going to make some waves...and this scared the living daylights out of me!

It wasn't until I was issued a challenge by a fire-and-brimstone preacher that I realized that as a Christian and a friend, it was time for me to lay aside my fear and get bold, no matter the cost. This preacher said one simple phrase that shook me to the core: "Picture your friends in hell."

One by one, I began to picture my friends in the water-sports world in that place of torment—friends who were so dear to me, friends with whom I had shared so many incredible experiences throughout the years. The pictures broke my heart. Seeing my friends in that horrific and very real place caused a great love to grow in my heart that exceeded the fear that had held me back.

What kind of friend was I if I refused to share the love of God and the truth of His Word because of fear? Not one at all.

In the fall of 2001, while driving in my car, I began to pray for God to help me have the courage to do what He was asking. I also asked Him to show me how He wanted me to carry out this mission. Within moments of saying this prayer, the idea of sharing my faith with the world of water-skiing through a written tract came to my mind.

Even though I was fairly certain that this was an instruction straight from God, I immediately began to question the soundness of the idea. My first doubt was regarding the effectiveness of a tract at a water-ski event. In those days, most events were sponsored by beer companies and attended by water-ski fans who were there to have fun and enjoy the performances on the water. I was quite positive that no one there wanted to hear about Jesus! Surely the people would just throw the tracts on the ground and trample over them. It would be a waste of resources.

Next, there was the issue that I had never written a thing in my life outside of school assignments; nor did I know anything about designing and publishing a tract. Finally, I threw out the financial argument. Surely having something designed and printed would be too costly and time consuming. How could all this be accomplished?

After a few hours of mentally wrestling with God, I decided I had a choice: I could either directly disobey God by not doing the tract or lay aside my "how" and "what if" questions and simply begin to write, trusting that He would help me. Praise God, I found the courage to choose the latter. And as I stepped out in faith, true to His Word, He took care of every detail.

I began by writing my own testimony. Then I interviewed other Christian professional water-sport athletes who graciously shared theirs. I was shocked at how quickly and easily the words began to flow out of my heart and onto the page. With the testimonies completed, all I needed was a title. As I prayed about what to call this God project, the words "Making the Cut" immediately popped into my head. They were perfect.

With everything done on my end, I went to my dad and shared the idea of *Making the Cut*. If you remember, my dad owned Overton's, the world's largest mail-order water-sports business. He had just what I needed: vast knowledge of the printing industry and an in-house graphic design team—something I had forgotten about when I was arguing with God about the validity of His idea. My dad graciously gave me access to his art department, which designed a beautiful, eye-catching, twenty-four-page, full-color booklet. Within a couple of months of this impression rising up in my heart, *Making the Cut* was complete and ready for distribution at the first professional event in April of 2002. It was truly amazing.

In 2002, we handed out fifteen thousand copies of *Making the Cut* at various water-sports events. People were literally lining up to get them. And you know what? In all the years I have distributed the booklet, I have never once seen one on the ground. Oh, me of little faith!

I have to smile as I think back to all my doubts and questions. I also have to smile as I think about God's provision and creativity. He thought of everything, all the way down to the tiniest of details. For example, the title, *Making the Cut*, that popped into my head, was a title that immediately attracted people to the booklet. People assumed it was a publication that was going to teach them how to make the cut on a water ski or wakeboard. Little did they know they were going to learn how to make the cut to Heaven.

Furthermore, the high-action pictures that were donated by various professional photographers also attracted water-ski and wakeboard fans. People wanted *Making the Cut*, as it contained pictures of their favorite athletes and made a perfect autograph piece. It was so awesome to watch people read the booklets on the shoreline as they waited for the athletes to perform. I knew that, although they had been attracted to *Making the Cut* because of the title and cool pictures, people would soon be drawn to Christ through the words of faith presented through the athletes' testimonies. And I was right.

After each event, I received letters telling me how this little booklet had impacted lives. People began asking me to send them copies so that they could distribute them as well. It wasn't long before I had to print more. In the next couple of years, tens of thousands of the *Making the Cut* tracts were distributed.

One of my favorite testimonies was from an inmate who had discovered a copy of *Making the Cut* in the cell where he had been placed for solitary confinement. This young man, once a surfer, was immediately attracted to the testimonies of the water-sports athletes. As he read their stories, God began to tug at his heart and reveal His great love for this young man. This man committed his life to Christ right there in that prison cell.

I have no idea how the tract got into that solitary place—it was intended for water-sports venues!—but isn't it wonderful that God isn't limited by our intentions? Isn't it also wonderful to know that God sees us wherever we are, even in a place of solitary confinement, and is willing to reach down into that place and reveal His love to us? Isn't it amazing that He will place people and even things like a *Making the Cut* tract into our paths to bring us into a relationship with Him? He loves us that much!

After the publication of *Making the Cut*, random thoughts about writing a book began to roam around my head. Once again, doubts and questions entered my mind. What kind of book would the Lord have me write? A daily devotional? An autobiography? I truly had no clue.

With no clear answer, I decided to lay aside my questions and simply start to write. As I sat before God each day, asking Him to write through me, my mind began to flow with analogies between my faith and the sport of water-skiing. Everywhere I looked, ordinary things like boats, vests, waves, and ski ropes suddenly took on spiritual meanings.

After months of writing, I looked back over my notes. Much to my amazement, each analogy could be grouped into specific categories that evolved into chapters. Right before my eyes, God had put this book together. All I had done was be obedient to sit and write what He placed on my heart.

With the manuscript complete, I thought to myself, "Now what?" This question would soon be answered in a most incredible way.

Within days of finishing the book, I received a phone call from a man named Jim. Jim, a boat dealer in Tennessee, had been distributing *Making the Cut* at his dealership as a witnessing tool to his customers for the past year. He explained to me that recently, a man who worked for a large Christian publishing company had come into the dealership and picked up the tract. Evidently interested in the publication, he asked who had produced it and if they had any other publications. Jim had passed on my information to this man, and a few days later, the man from the publishing company called. He wanted to know if I had any other writings.

Well, it just so happened that I had a freshly finished manuscript lying right on my desk. I couldn't believe my ears when he asked me to overnight it to him along with an outline and a one-page summary. The next thing I knew, I had a contract with one of the largest Christian publishing companies in the world for a beautiful, full-color, hardback book called *Running the Course*.

Isn't God something? I am in total awe as I look back at how He pieces people and things together in our lives. He places dreams in our hearts and ideas in our heads and then makes a way to do what we could never do on our own.

SOMETHING TO THINK ABOUT

God isn't looking for people who have all the answers, money, special talents, and unique skills to accomplish His work. He isn't looking for performers who can bring it all to fruition. Rather, He is searching the world for one thing—a willing heart that will simply reply, "Yes, Lord. I'll do it!" even when it doesn't understand how, why, when, or what.

God once revealed this very lesson through my young daughter, Ivy, while we were ministering together in Russia. (You'll meet Ivy in Chapter 12.) During our two-week stay, there were many times when Ivy wanted to know every detail about our day trips. She'd ask where we were going, why we had to go, when we'd return home, how long it would take, and who would be at our destination before she would actually get in the car. Repeatedly, with snow falling on my head, I would ask her to get in the car. Yet her questions would continue.

Finally, my frustration mounting, I looked at her and said, "Ivy, you don't have to know every detail to move. Just get in the car! Trust that we know where we are going and we will take care of you."

All of a sudden, God slapped my heart with the truth that we, His children, are often like my precious Ivy. We want to know all the details before we decide to get in the car with Him. We stand outside repeatedly asking, "Where are we going, Lord? How long is it going to take? How are we going to get there? Why are we going this way? Why is it taking so long?"

Sometimes God answers our questions but sometimes He doesn't, at least not in the timing or way we'd like. I can just picture God saying to us (surely with more patience than I exhibited), "Just get in the car, My child. You don't have to know everything to move forward. Just be still and know that I AM the answer to all of your questions."

I agree—it's usually more comfortable to know the details. Yet as I look back over my life, I can say with all certainty—details or no details, God has faithfully guided me to my destination and fulfilled every promise, desire, and dream He has placed in my heart. Through my willingness, He has gone to work, orchestrating events, resources, and opportunities to bring about the very thing He called me to do. And He'll do the same for you.

CHAPTER 9

IN HIS WAKES

*"And you must love the Lord your God with all your heart,
all your soul, all your mind, and all your strength." The
second is equally important: "Love your neighbor as yourself."
No other commandment is greater than these.*

MARK 12:30–31

With my faith fueled by the impact of the *Making the Cut* tract and God's miraculous provision for the publication of *Running the Course*, my focus began to shift from bringing home gold medals to touching lives for Christ through the sport I loved. Being the current world record holder, I had an incredible platform. As I competed on tour, I continued to hold worship services at various water-ski events as well as distribute the *Making the Cut* tract, all the while dreaming a new vision of impacting lives—especially youth—outside of our sport.

Water-skiing had taught me so many wonderful life lessons about faith, perseverance, integrity, goal setting, teamwork, and discipline. I knew without a doubt, if given the opportunity, water sports could greatly teach others these same principles as well as influence their physical, emotional, and spiritual health.

With this vision burning in my heart, I officially established a nonprofit organization called "In His Wakes" (IHW). Its mission? To introduce people to the life-changing power of Jesus Christ through water sports.

Propelled by a heart full of passion, I set out to fulfill the above mission. In addition to ministering to water-sports enthusiasts through the tract and worship services, In His Wakes would now reach people outside the sport through two programs: a faith-based water-ski show called "The Night of Champions," and a unique outreach called "A Day to Remember."

The Night of Champions (NOC) ski shows were absolutely amazing and so much fun to organize and participate in. They were exceptional in that they showcased the talents of top athletes from every aspect of our sport—show skiing, traditional three-event skiing, knee boarding, wake boarding, and barefooting—and combined them with powerful testimonies of the athletes' faith. As athletes from around the world shared the True Source of their strength, many people gave their lives to Christ. Over fifteen thousand people attended these exciting and impactful events during the two years they were held at various locations across the country.

Although the events were well attended and strongly supported financially by top water-sports manufacturers, I realized by the end of 2004 that the ministry's focus needed to shift from presenting the elaborate water-sports shows to building the "Day to Remember" (D2R) program. The D2R was unarguably an incredible vessel that God was using to not only touch people's lives but to transform them.

Unlike the NOC, the D2R ministers to people on an intimate, individual level. Through the hands-on water-sports activities, such as swimming, water-skiing, knee boarding, and tubing, relationships are built that create opportunities to not only teach people new skills but also to show them the love of God in a unique and tangible way.

When the participants experience victory doing an activity that most consider impossible (especially since 80 percent of our participants cannot swim), a powerful connection is made for God's love to be demonstrated, shared, and received. The D2R is more than a ski-day. It is a day when lives are literally transformed.

A favorite success story from the D2R program involves a young girl named Amber. Her victory is a perfect example of why I am so passionate about the D2R events. When I first met Amber, a resident of Chick-fil-A's

WinShape Homes, she, like many of our participants, was extremely fearful of the water and stubbornly hesitant to ski. Now, I can coax most kids out of their comfort zones fairly quickly, but not Amber. No amount of prompting or bribing from me or any member of our team could get her to move out of the boat and into water-skis.

As I continued to push Amber in love, I began to pray. "Lord, show me how to get this little girl to trust me. She needs to get up on those skis!"

Like many of our participants, fear had a death grip on this child, and I knew it needed to be broken—not for the sake of her learning to ski, but so she could experience true freedom in life. If fear was controlling her on the water, it was most likely controlling her in other areas.

God answered my prayer by giving me these words, "Amber, if you'd like to ski, I'll help you—and you won't even get wet!"

Evidently, God knew these were the very words this little girl needed to hear for her to have the confidence to move past her fear. They certainly weren't words I would have spoken otherwise. Why would I make an impossible promise like this? A key ingredient in water-skiing is water, and water is wet!

To my surprise, Amber replied with a huge smile, "Okay!"

While Amber made her way to the side of the boat and began to put on her skis, I prayed once again, "Lord, help me carry out this promise."

In a moment's flash, I saw a mental image of my body stretched out of the side of the boat, snaked around the boom that we use to teach beginner skiers. With my body securely twisted around the horizontal bar, I saw Amber sitting safely on my forearms, well above the water.

After explaining to her what I was going to do, Amber courageously grabbed hold of the boom and sat on my forearm as I lifted her small frame above the water. I told the boat driver to "hit it," and off we went. With my help and a lot of help from above, little Amber skied circles around the lake without ever getting wet!

No victory I've ever experienced as a world champion skier can even come close to the thrill of witnessing Amber skim across the top of the water. Tears stung my eyes as she waved to her peers who were cheering her on from the shoreline.

Later in the day, Amber's guardian shared with me the source of Amber's fear. It stemmed from her mother's abusive act of actually trying to drown Amber as punishment. Due to this horrific incident, Amber had been deathly afraid of water—until our event. On *that* day, through the simple sport of water-skiing, God set little Amber free.

By the end of our event, Amber was swimming underwater, completely unafraid. And in the months that followed, her guardian reported that Amber overcame other emotional barriers in school and other areas of her life, all as a result of what she learned and experienced through the D2R. Talk about victory!

This is just one of thousands of stories where God has used the sport I love to bring hope, healing, and victory into the lives of people who are so precious to Him but so often overlooked by the world. Amber's face, and those of thousands of other children, are forever etched into my heart and mind. They are a constant inspiration to me to get off the dock and face my own fears!

Once the ministry's focus turned to developing the D2R outreach, God greatly expanded the territory of IHW. What began in 2003 as a program with a few Florida and North Carolina events is now a sixty-event national tour conducted by two teams. IHW has even traveled overseas to work with children in the Czech Republic, Costa Rica, and Austria. To date, more than twenty thousand people have heard the gospel of Jesus Christ and been encouraged to "get off the dock" and follow Him through the various IHW programs.

Something to Think About

Has God asked you to step out into unfamiliar territory? Like Amber, has He asked you to face a situation that in the past nearly destroyed you and left you for dead? Or, like me, has God laid a vision on your heart that seems greater than your abilities or resources?

If so, then it's time to move. It's time to *GET OFF THE DOCK!* It's time to face your fears and questions and insecurities and just simply move out onto the water with Christ. Why? Because victory only comes when you are willing to get off the dock. Breakthrough and healing are realized when you thrust yourself out into the deep, trusting the One who calls you out.

Often when God puts visions in our hearts and opportunities in our paths, we tend to come up with a hundred and one reasons why we should stay in our comfort zones. Rather than focusing on God and trusting His power and provision, we focus on the things we expect to be a hindrance to our success—things like money, people, the economy, our education, gender, experience (or lack thereof), or our past.

But you know what? With God, there are no hindrances, and there is no lack.

Friend, if God has placed something on your heart, then trust Him. He who has begun that good work in you will carry it to completion. God is faithful. Whatever you need, He will supply—so move! What you perceive as lack is a nonissue. The Lord is your Shepherd, and He will protect you, guide you in your decisions, and provide for your every need. According to Psalm 23, you will never lack a thing! The only hindrance to victory is your own unwillingness to step out in faith. So step out. *Be strong and of good courage, do not fear or be in dread…for it is the Lord your God who goes with you; He will not fail you or forsake you (Deuteronomy 31:6 RSV).*

CHAPTER 10

LESSONS FROM LA-LA
LAND

Each time he said, "My grace is all you need.
My power works best in weakness." So now I am glad to boast
about my weaknesses, so that the power of
Christ can work through me.

2 CORINTHIANS 12:9

With each child's victory, my heart grew increasingly passionate about giving more children the opportunity to experience the D2R program. It was obvious to me that full-time ministry through In His Wakes was the new direction God intended for my life. Working with these children brought me so much joy and gave eternal purpose to my water-skiing talents. So, without abandon, I focused intently on growing the ministry and making it a success.

With a reduction in professional tour events due to a declining economy, and less time on the water due to increased physical pain, I was able to give more of my time and energy to developing IHW. After only a year of organizing events, however, my physical pain grew to a level that required medical attention. Interestingly, it wasn't my recent neck fusion or previous stomach issues that were causing the intolerable pain, it was a congenital hip disorder.

Since I was a teenager, I had known that my hip sockets had not developed properly. The problem was first discovered as I played soccer during my sophomore year of high school. Due to the large amounts of running required in soccer, my hips were constantly aggravated and became painfully inflamed.

Initial x-rays in 1986 revealed that the top of my femur bone was 80 percent outside of my hip sockets. The only thing holding my bones in place were the strong leg muscles I had developed through decades of water-skiing. In search of relief, my parents and I had flown to Utah to consult with one of the country's top hip surgeons.

Due to the complexity of the surgery required to reconstruct my pelvis, the surgeon warned us that if I elected to have the operation, my ski career would most likely be over. I was only sixteen years old and at the top of my sport. This was news neither I nor my parents wanted to hear.

After prayer and discussion, we decided to hold off on the surgery and instead, stop doing the things that aggravated my hips, such as soccer, basketball, and other high-impact sports. We also made adjustments on the water to reduce my pain level. For example, I began to focus more on the slalom event, since it was lower impact and required less hip movement than the trick and jump events. These changes gave me longevity in the sport.

From 1986 until 2003, by the grace of God, I managed to press through my hip pain and ski victoriously. But not anymore. My body was screaming, "Enough!"

Although only thirty-three years old, my body simply could no longer do what my brain willed it to do, no matter how hard I tried. Event after event, I struggled to press on to victory, to no avail. As the pain increased, it was clear that my professional skiing days had come to an end, and the pelvic surgery I had been putting off since high school was upon me.

Reluctantly, I started searching for a surgeon who would be able to perform the surgery I needed. There were a few qualified doctors in Florida, but their experience dealing with cases such as mine was extremely limited. As I researched my options, I became discouraged. One day as I flew home from a ministry event, I looked out the window, over the clouds, and cried out to God, "Lord, please show me what to do."

Within a couple of days, I had an answer to my prayer. The phone rang, and from the other end of the line came these words. "Kristi, this is Dr. Michael Millis, an orthopedic surgeon from the Children's Hospital in Boston. I hear you need my services."

I was in shock. I had not contacted this doctor, nor had I instructed anyone else to contact him. In fact, I had never even heard of him. It turned out that Dr. Millis specialized in the Ganz Osteotomy, the procedure I required. In fact, he was a world-renowned expert in his field, and he was calling me! By the end of our conversation, we had scheduled an appointment for me to meet him in Boston the next week. Isn't God amazing?

When I entered the doors of that hospital in January 2004, I was overwhelmed with peace. I knew God had brought me to this place and that He would continue to care for me through whatever I had to face. By the end of the day, I had met with Dr. Millis, taken numerous x-rays and MRIs, and began to store blood for my first operation that was a mere two weeks away. We also made plans for the second and third operations in July and November of that same year.

It was a miracle in itself that Dr. Millis had called me, but there were some other blessings as well. I was thirty-four years old at the time. The cut-off age for having surgery at the Children's Hospital was thirty-five. I would be able to have all three surgeries that year at the same hospital under Dr. Millis and his staff's care. Furthermore, my father had just sold Overtons, and my insurance was in the last stages of COBRA. I would be able to have all the surgeries on my pelvis under this policy. Talk about a huge blessing.

Thirty years after my career began, I headed to Boston Children's Hospital to undergo a total reconstruction of my pelvis. Since my hip sockets had failed to develop, the surgery would require the left side of my pelvis (and in six months, my right) to be cut in several places so that Dr. Millis could rotate my hip socket and create a covering for my femoral head. At the conclusion of the nine-hour operation, six metal pins would be inserted to hold the pelvis in its new position while the bones fused together. Both the first and second surgeries would require me to be totally non-weight-bearing for three months. How thankful I was that God only gave me two hips!

It was a long recovery, but during that journey, blessings abounded. First of all, I witnessed a side of Tim that I never knew existed. He proved through his loving actions that he was indeed committed to our marriage "in sickness and in health." Day after day, he performed not-so-glamorous tasks like emptying my excretions, washing out the handicap toilet that sat by our bed, lifting me in and out of the bathtub, holding me upright in the shower, and bathing my body. My love for him grew as I witnessed his love expressed in tender ways, like when he would repeatedly rearrange my pillows under my legs until they were just perfect.

Another blessing was the revelation I received regarding some weaknesses in my personality that were hindering my walk with the Lord as well as my relationships with others. You know, trials have a way of exposing those not-so-pretty areas of our lives. A wise friend once said to me, "When rain pours down, trash will somehow find its way to the top." How true! I am reminded of this analogy every time I walk past a retention pond in my neighborhood after a downpour. Without fail, trash is always floating on the surface—trash I had never noticed before the rain.

During my recovery period, some *trash* rose to the surface of my life. One weakness revealed was my inability to rest. (I'm still fighting this one!) I had an incredibly difficult time staying in bed and allowing my body time to recover. I pushed myself to continue all my normal activities as I fought an urgent need to be productive. Surely I needed to be doing more than just recovering from surgery. Wasn't that pure laziness? To a Type A personality, yes, it was.

Another weakness revealed was my inability to ask for help. Rather than risk bothering someone, I usually attempted to do everything myself. The problem with this, I quickly learned, was that it was impossible to do everything, much less to do everything well. Eventually I collapsed under the weight of the pressure I placed on myself to keep going at full speed. Furthermore, by shutting people out, I prevented many people from receiving the blessing of being able to help our family.

I didn't realize how stubborn I was until the day I scooted across the kitchen floor on my stomach (as I couldn't put any weight on my hip) so that I could pick up a small crumb on the carpet. During this whole fiasco, Tim was sitting just a few feet from me at the kitchen table. With each painful movement, I began to fume inwardly. I couldn't understand why he didn't see that crumb and just pick it up, for goodness' sake!

When I finally couldn't take the pain any longer, I collapsed facedown on the floor and yelled, "Can't you see I need some help?"

Tim just looked at me and calmly replied, "I just wanted to see how far you'd go before you'd ask for my help."

What a reply! He might just as well have hit me over the head with my crutch! I quickly learned the importance of communication (a discipline I'm still trying to master). As one who doesn't want to offend anyone, I don't like asking people to do something. I'd rather them just see it and do it, whatever it is. Yet at the same time, I somehow expect those people to know exactly what needs to be done and to do it promptly. If they don't, I grow frustrated and even angry.

That's not really fair, is it? It's not fair to my husband, children, friends, or those whom I've been called to lead in ministry. The fact is, people are different, and no, much to my dismay, they don't necessarily see things the same way I do; nor do they have the same priorities. Therefore, it's better for everyone if expectations are laid out in love.

My recovery period taught me things about myself and my marriage, but it also showed me my role within the ministry. I learned very quickly that IHW is about more than where I can be and what I can do. It is about the body of Christ working together for God's glory.

The second pelvic reconstruction procedure was approaching, and I couldn't quite understand God's timing in relation to the IHW ministry. Why would He lead me to start this project, only to allow circumstances to take me from it? So much hard work had gone into setting up and promoting this organization. Wouldn't it lose momentum if I suddenly stepped away?

I learned that not only would it not lose momentum, it would actually expand at an incredible rate. The secret to the expansion? Having to rely on God and others to carry out the vision He had placed in my heart. No longer was the ministry limited to where I could be and what I could do. During my recovery, I had no choice but to relinquish control if there were to be any D2R events anywhere other than my home states of Florida and North Carolina. Since I was unable to travel, I agreed to allow several trustworthy people to host their own D2R events.

I remember this scene like it was yesterday. There I was, lying on my parents' couch, floating in and out of la-la land—you know, that drug-induced place you visit when you are recovering from surgery. Over and over again, my cell phone rang as these trusted national D2R hosts called to share their praise reports.

First, I received a call from South Carolina. "Kristi, I wish you could have been here," Melinda Rodgers said through tears. "It was incredible! We had all these children from an emergency domestic violence shelter. Some had just been brought to the shelter during the night. Boy, did they need this day on the water!"

Then came calls from Texas, Colorado, and California with similar reports. Finally, I received a call from Minnesota that radically changed our ministry. "Kristi, we had over sixty Hispanic participants at our event! We shared the gospel, and a majority of the kids received Christ as their Savior!"

Until this time, I had not given D2R participants the opportunity to accept Christ as their Savior and Lord. Rather, I had focused on giving the kids an incredible experience on the water, providing warm hospitality, and presenting them with a goodie bag complete with a T-shirt, a *Making the Cut* tract, an inscribed gold medal, my *Running the Course* book, and a Bible.

"I don't want to push the gospel on these kids," I reasoned to myself. "I'll just bring them out to the lake, give them an incredible experience on the water, pray before we eat our tasty Chick-fil-A sandwiches, share an encouraging message about being a champion, and send them home with faith-based materials. If they want to, they can discover how to be a Christian in my book or the tract or, of course, in the Bible."

God used the host in Minnesota to reveal my remaining fear of sharing Christ with others, even children. He also showed me how, once again, my people-pleasing tendencies were causing me to forfeit an incredible opportunity to share Christ with people whose hearts were ripe for the harvest.

After learning about the impact of the Minnesota event, I committed to share the gospel at every future D2R event. Regardless of what organization we were partnering with, I determined that Christ would remain the focus. Because of this commitment, hundreds of children have made public professions of faith. Many have even asked to be baptized at our events.

During that week in la-la land, God showed up! He not only sustained the ministry during my recovery, but He expanded its territory, using others to continue the vision of IHW. I have to smile when I consider the fact that during that week, more events were conducted while I laid on the couch than in the previous year while I ran at full speed!

Experiencing God's faithfulness in my health and the ministry gave me the confidence and peace to officially retire from the sport I loved in May of 2005. Although my ski career had ended, I looked forward with excitement to the next new season of life.

SOMETHING TO THINK ABOUT

When God placed the vision of In His Wakes on my heart, I erroneously believed that I had to make that vision a success. During my recovery period, however, I humbly realized that God really didn't need little ole me to carry out His plans for In His Wakes.

God showed me through the D2R hosts that there were many people capable of carrying out the vision of In His Wakes. He also showed me that, regardless of my weaknesses (in this case physical), He would continue to move this ministry forward. My responsibility wasn't to make things happen. It was to simply trust God and to be a willing vessel through which His love could flow. What a relief!

Is there anything in your life that you feel responsible to make a success? Have you considered asking God to help you?

CHAPTER 11

FAITH THAT MOVES MOUNTAINS, PART 1

God has not given us a spirit of fear and timidity,
but of power, love, and self-discipline.
2 TIMOTHY 1:7

During 2003, my first year of official ministry with In His Wakes, I had begun to mention to Tim my desire to adopt children. This desire had been in my heart since I was a young child. Now that we, through our ministry, were interacting with children, some of whom were orphaned and in the foster care system, this desire was growing stronger and stronger by the day.

My desire was deep, but at first, Tim's wasn't. He knew our life was already full of commitments and activities. We had tried for more children naturally, but to no avail. Tim seemed quite content with one child, but I longed for more. Ty, now six years old, was quickly growing, and I wanted him to experience the joys and trials of having siblings while he was young.

For months I brought up the subject of adoption with Tim. Our discussions seemed to be going nowhere. So, I handed over my desire to God. I asked Him to either change my heart or change Tim's. I didn't want to nag Tim to death or push him into a decision. Boy, had I come a long way! But I also didn't want to go through life with this insatiable desire. Something had to give.

If we adopted, I longed to adopt a child from Russia. I had traveled to Russia during my professional water-ski career, and my heart seemed to be drawn there. I shared my desire with a few close friends and asked them to pray for God's will to prevail.

In the fall of 2003, I was in North Carolina for a signing event for my newly released book, *Running the Course*. While there, a close friend gave me a pamphlet from an adoption agency located in Austin, Texas. She and her husband had considered adopting, but with the unexpected birth of their third son, they had decided to wait.

When I returned to Florida, I called the agency and asked them to mail me an application. Perhaps one day Tim would change his mind, and when he did, I would be ready. The application sat on my desk, untouched, for several months—until the night before I left for Boston to go have my pelvis reconstructed.

I was sitting at my desk making last-minute arrangements for my trip when Tim walked in and said, "I've been thinking about this adoption thing, and you're right. Let's adopt, and let's get two!" Better be careful what you pray for!

God had answered my prayers. He had changed Tim's heart and brought us into unity. The timing seemed a little off, at least in my opinion, but that didn't stop me from signing on the dotted line and sticking the application in the mail before we flew out to Boston for my surgery.

As you've already read, the surgeries and recovery period proved to be quite challenging. But they served to prepare both Tim and me for the challenges that would arise during our adoption. In the following pages, I'd like to share our adoption experience. It may seem strange that I would devote more time to our one-and-a-half-year adoption experience than my thirty-year career on the water as a professional athlete, but the fact is, this adoption experience catapulted Tim and me to an entirely new level of faith. It brought us closer to each other and to God than anything else we had ever experienced.

Here is our story.

After my first hip surgery in January 2004, with my initial application already completed and forwarded to the agency, I spent a lot of time learning about international adoptions. The whole process was so foreign to me. (Sorry, I couldn't resist!) Unless you have engaged in this process yourself, you cannot begin to understand the mass of paperwork that prospective adoptive families must fill out. It is an incredibly lengthy and tedious process with many twists and turns.

Due to all the uncertainties with my second and third operations, all scheduled for that same year, we had only sent our initial application to the Austin adoption agency, acknowledging our intent to adopt. They, in turn, had mailed us a large packet of information and a checklist of sorts. Being the Type A person that I am, I immediately completed the paperwork, even though I had months of therapy and another surgery to undergo before we could even consider adopting. This inch-thick stack of papers sat neatly piled on my desk, just like the other stack, for months…six months to be exact.

One day in August, a month after my second surgery, a friend from Colorado visited our home. She asked me about our adoption process. I told her I had filled out at least the first wave of the necessary paperwork but was waiting until my November surgery to send it in. I didn't want to get too deep into the process and get called by the agency to go meet a child. What if I couldn't travel?

In the midst of listing my excuses, Michele shocked me with these words. "Kristi, don't you think God knows everything you have to go through? Don't you think you can trust Him with the details of this adoption?"

It was the best slap in the face I could have ever had. Don't you just love friends who can be brutally honest with you? I do, as long as their words are backed by love, truth, and encouragement. As I pondered her question, I realized my not moving forward in this adoption wasn't because God had told me to hold back, it was because of fear. I was afraid of what might happen if I sent in the papers.

At that moment, with truth staring me in the face, I decided to trust God completely. Tim and I discussed the issue and decided we would send in the paperwork the very next day.

What happened next is nothing short of a miracle. When we finished discussing this, I went to soak my ailing hips. While I was still in the bathtub, the phone rang. Suddenly, Tim came running into the bathroom and handed me the phone. "It's the agency!" he exclaimed. "They have a child for us!"

The representative from the agency wanted to know where I was in my recovery process. I explained to her I was still non-weight-bearing and had one more surgery scheduled in November.

"Kristi," she said, "we have gone through all of our applicants, and we keep coming back to your family's application. We feel without a doubt that this child is supposed to be in your family."

The timing of her call was miraculous, but the truly amazing thing was that the paperwork required to receive such a referral was still sitting on my desk. This referral, received just moments after our decision to trust God, would normally take months, even after all the required paperwork had been submitted.

As I looked at my scarred, throbbing body in the tub, I laid aside any fear of the timing of this call and simply said, "Thank you, God!" The next day, true to our word, we mailed off the paperwork to the agency.

Over the next few months, we were in constant contact with the agency as we awaited our invitation to go meet our little boy, Denis. During that time, we received a picture of him through our email. It was love at first sight.

When Ty, my blue-eyed, blond-haired son saw the picture of this dark-haired, black-eyed little boy, he yelled out, "He looks just like me, Mama! He looks just like me!"

Along with the coveted picture came some vital information. Denis was almost four years old. His mother had been raised in the same orphanage as Denis, and she had three children, her first at age twelve. The oldest child had been adopted by his mother's family, but Denis and his younger brother, Misha, had been raised in the orphanage. We also found out that Misha had recently been adopted by a family in the Midwest that *just so happened* to have used the same agency in Austin that we were using. How thankful I am that God prompted my friend in North Carolina to give me the brochure of this agency!

Since adoptions are closed (meaning that information of the child and adoptive family is protected by law), Misha's family had voluntarily given permission for their contact information to be revealed in the case that Denis was referred to a family through their agency. The chances of this were slim, as there are many agencies. Denis could have been adopted by any number of families from across the world. Once again, my God showed that He is a God against all odds.

I quickly contacted Todd and Bonnie Hagemann per their request. Misha's mother Bonnie and I became fast friends. Not only did we share a connection with these precious boys, but we shared a common faith, values, and work ethic. As she shared about their adoption journey, it was quite obvious that God's plan included bringing our families together. We were, in fact, an answer to Bonnie's prayers.

Todd and Bonnie had actually planned to adopt Denis. Just like us, they had received a phone call to go meet Denis, their future son. But God had other plans for Denis and his brother. Just as the Hagemanns were going to Russia to meet Denis, Bonnie prayed, "Lord, if this isn't the child You desire for us to have, please make it known."

When they arrived in Russia, God gave Bonnie and Todd their answer. It turns out that during their travel to Russia, Denis's mother suddenly came to visit him, but she didn't visit Misha, who was located just across the hall. Her visit caused Denis to be unavailable for adoption by the

Hagemanns. It also started the long waiting period of his being able to be adopted by any family all over again.

When the Hagemanns arrived to meet Denis, rather than meeting him, they were introduced to his younger brother, Misha, who was eighteen months old. The Hagemanns accepted this little boy with love into their family, knowing that God was in control, but their hearts still ached for Denis. When they returned home, they gathered a team of believers to pray for Denis, asking specifically for him to be adopted by a Christian family who would be open to having the boys reunited. God answered her prayers and the silent prayers of these two brothers who should have been forever separated.

The Hagemanns helped us tremendously during our adoption process. It was so difficult waiting for our official invitation to travel to Russia. How wonderful it was to have a family who not only had been through the same process but who had also experienced God's faithfulness. They consistently spurred us on! Bonnie and I grew closer with each phone call. We were, after all, mothers of brothers.

November rolled around with no news of an invitation to Russia. I was kind of relieved, because my third pelvic surgery was scheduled during that month. It was time to return to Boston to get those aggravating, constricting pins out of my right hip.

God is so amazing. The day I promised to trust Him with the details of my surgery, He blessed Tim and I with the referral of a son. Just two weeks after my last surgery and two days after I shed my crutches, we received our invitation to fly to Russia and meet our son.

Tim and I were so excited about this opportunity to travel, but our hearts were still torn because we had not been given a referral for a little girl. We both felt strongly that God was leading us to adopt both a little girl and a little boy at the same time.

We were given the choice: we could travel to Russia in four days, or we could wait for a referral for a little girl. I was not about to make this little boy wait any longer for a family. Little Denis was already almost four years old. He had lived in an orphanage most of his life and had already witnessed all of his friends and his brother leave the orphanage with families. It was time for him to come home.

With our decision to travel, life went into high gear, real fast. That's part of the excitement of an international adoption. As an adopting family, there is simply no way to predict when the call to travel will arrive—and when it does, you have only days to prepare. Within four days of our invitation, we finalized papers in Tallahassee, purchased plane tickets to Russia, expedited our passports to the Russian Embassy in order to obtain visas, arranged childcare for Ty, hired dogsitters, and, of course, packed.

Praise God, everything worked together for good just as promised in Romans 8:28. We received our Fed-Ex package complete with passports and visas the morning of our flight. As we headed off to meet our little boy, I tucked away in my heart all the examples of God's faithfulness over the past years. He had been with me during every surgery, and He had worked out every detail and the timing of this adoption. I knew without a doubt He would be with us now and with our precious son, Ty, whom we were leaving behind. We had no idea what lay ahead in Russia, but fortunately for us, we knew the One who did.

SOMETHING TO THINK ABOUT

We often hold back in life because we are afraid. Fear is never a reason to back down from what you sense God is calling you to do. As you've seen, I've allowed fear to keep me from sharing my faith, and it almost kept me from trusting God for my children. Yet when I laid aside my fear, miraculous things happened.

A spirit of fear does not come from God. Yes, God may use His Holy Spirit to warn you, perhaps to cause you to back away from someone or something. But His Spirit will never bring doubt, confusion, or anxiety.

The spirit of fear comes only from Satan. More than anything, he wants to kill, steal, and destroy what is rightfully yours. He wants you curled up on the edge, stuck on the dock of life; and he'll use anything—fear, anger, guilt, shame, your insecurities—to keep you there. Don't give him the victory! Cast all your fears on Christ, and trust Him with all your uncertainties.

CHAPTER 12

FAITH THAT MOVES
MOUNTAINS, PART 2

For nothing is impossible with God.
LUKE 1:37

In November 2004, we arrived in Moscow and were greeted by representatives of the adoption agency that worked closely with our Austin agency. They took us to the Hotel Ukraina in the heart of the city where we would rest until the next day. We weren't given a lot of information other than, "Someone will pick you up tomorrow." Talk about moments requiring trust.

True to their word, someone did come to get us. They escorted us to a local airport so we could catch a flight to the region where Denis was located. When we boarded the plane, we were a bit taken aback by the condition of the aircraft. My father is a pilot with his jet rating, and I knew if he could see us, he'd have a heart attack! This aircraft, covered in snow, looked like it had been resurrected from an American aviation graveyard.

As I entered the rear of the aircraft (that's right, the rear), I watched with horror as two men swept a foot of snow off the wings of the plane with a broom and then used a flimsy water hose to drizzle some type of antifreeze fluid on the wings. With snow falling heavily outside, I simply prayed over and over again, "Lord, I trust You." I had no choice but to lay aside my fear and rely on the truth that God had called us to adopt this child, and He had worked out every detail. Surely, He would not forget about us now.

The interior of the plane resembled the inside of an old bus. The seats faced each other, and the luggage was kept overhead on open metal racks. The windows had bright orange curtains that closed from the sides. Above my head, I discovered a button that actually said "stewardess" that I could press in case I needed assistance—not that anyone would understand me.

Safety was obviously not a priority. Several passengers walked up and down the aisles during takeoff, passing out small white cups to one another to hold the vodka that they were sharing. Perhaps they figured it would kill the pain if the plane went down!

Fortunately, we arrived in the region safely and were met by a handsome gentleman named Alexander. He spotted us right away. Could it have been our four extra-large, bright blue duffel bags embroidered with water-skiers? Or perhaps the relieved look on our faces to be off the plane? Alexander took us to a small room where we stayed for the night.

The next morning, we were picked up by our translator and the adoption facilitator. These nice ladies took care of us every remaining step of the way. After receiving an official invitation from the Ministry of Education to enter the orphanage, Tim and I climbed into a car and headed down a bumpy, frozen highway to meet Denis.

Once at the orphanage, we were escorted to the office of the orphanage director, Dr. Stalina. Through a translator, she gave us a brief medical overview of Denis's health. Then we were led upstairs to his room. It was an incredible moment. Denis had just awakened from a nap and was a bit confused as to what was going on. After a small snack and a pep talk from his caretakers, he wandered over to us with a little more excitement. I wasn't quite sure how to approach this small boy, but Tim reached right down and picked him up. After a few minutes, Denis climbed into my arms. I couldn't believe how light he was. He fit perfectly in my arms. He buried his face in my chest and then grabbed my necklace, which held a picture of Ty. I pointed to it and explained to him in bits of Russian that it was his brother. Denis just nodded and smiled.

As we walked down the halls of the orphanage, Denis excitedly told everyone that his mama and papa had come. They genuinely looked happy for him. He was the oldest child in the orphanage, and very special to these ladies. We played with Denis for about an hour before Dr. Stalina asked us if we'd like to adopt him. Without hesitation, Tim and I replied, "Yes!" and signed the papers.

After signing, we were told it was time to go, and we were escorted out the door. As I looked up from the car to the second-story orphanage window, little Denis was standing at the glass waving good-bye. Did he understand that we didn't want to leave him? Did he understand that we'd be back? Tears stung my eyes, and pain gripped my heart. I had to rely on my faith and trust that God knew what He was doing.

During our trip, we had continually requested a referral for a little girl. Over and over again, we were told that there were no little girls available. That evening when we returned to our hotel, I felt the Lord leading me to ask one more time. So I did.

The next morning, our adoption facilitator told us, through our translator, that she had some news for us. She opened up a large registry, a big notebook of sorts filled with pictures of Russian orphans. She looked at Tim and me and said, "It seems that a little girl has suddenly appeared."

The facilitator shared with us that this little girl, Veronika, lived in the nearby region in a children's hospital. She and her other siblings had been abandoned by their mother. The facilitator pointed to the brown-eyed little girl and said, "She looks just like her father." She was referring to Tim. She was right, she did resemble him. Once again, I was blown away by God's timing and provision.

After breakfast, we filled out official documents and headed down the icy highway to the children's hospital in Sarapul where Veronika resided. As we entered this run-down hospital, something gripped my heart. When we had met Denis, I experienced peace. Although he lived in an orphanage, he was obviously in a place where people loved him deeply and cared for him properly. He was a happy little boy, fairly well nourished and active beyond words. Here, I didn't have that same sense of peace.

When we arrived, we were quickly led to a private room where we were met by a very young male doctor. Without any emotion, he gave us Veronika's medical history.

Afterward, a frail, pale, little girl walked into the room. It's hard to explain how such a tiny frame could command such attention, but she did. She just filled the room with her presence. Mine and Tim's hearts immediately bonded to this little girl. This was our daughter, our promise from God fulfilled. Tim looked at her and lovingly said, "Hi, beautiful."

Within moments she was whispering the most beautiful words we had ever heard, "Mama. Papa." Our hearts just melted.

Too soon, it was time to go. We were given the opportunity to visit her briefly the next morning before returning to Moscow for our flight home. When we left, my heart ripped out of my chest. I cried all the way back to the airport. I just wanted to pack these kids up and take them home, but I couldn't. I had to leave them and once again trust that God would take care of them and reunite us in His perfect timing.

As we boarded the plane, we were told we'd be back very soon for our court date. What we thought would be a two-week turn-around, however, turned out to be a five-month wait. To make matters more trying, international adoptions were halted during those months, and we were told that our children could possibly be put up for adoption by Russian citizens. Again, I had to fight fear and go back to the truth…God was in control.

I prayed fervently for our children as I shed tears over our packed bags. I felt so helpless. There was absolutely nothing I could do but wait.

True to His word, God was faithful to protect our children, and in His perfect timing—April of 2005—we received the call to travel to Russia to adopt our children. When we walked through the orphanage doors in

Glazov, Russia, Denis and Veronika were waiting for us with open arms. (During our wait, Veronika had been transferred from the hospital to the orphanage where Denis resided. She had been living there for almost three months.)

As we spent the required four days of interaction with Denis and Veronika under the observation of a social worker, it became obvious that God had used these many months of waiting for good. These two children had truly bonded as siblings, and Veronika's physical health was obviously better—as was mine. During our court hearing, we learned how her time at the orphanage had enabled her to mature emotionally. Because of the neglect she had experienced early in her life, Veronika didn't know her name, nor did she speak a language. One caretaker told the judge that when she'd arrived at the orphanage, she had been like a wild animal.

Tim and I had no idea of the severity of her condition. Thank goodness, or we may have been too afraid to take on the challenge. I believe God, in His grace, shielded us from this information.

As I watched Denis and Veronika play together, I thanked God for the wait. I thanked Him for His perfect timing. What had been such a painful, difficult, and often confusing time had turned out to be exactly what we all needed. Had I been able to fix what I thought was broken, I would have surely made a mess of things.

Next to our marriage and Ty's birth, the day our adoption was declared official was one of the happiest days of our lives. As the judge pronounced Dalton Denis and Ivy Veronika part of the Johnson clan, Tim picked me up and swung me around. It had been quite a process; one that changed our lives forever.

God had given us this victory, and we weren't the only ones who recognized God's hand in the process. One of the witnesses in our adoption proceeding told the judge, "It is as if God has put this family together Himself." If only she knew.

SOMETHING TO THINK ABOUT

Years after our adoption experience, I was asking God to teach me how to have mountain-moving faith (Matthew 21:21). I had been studying in the Bible the amazing truth that our faith, our complete trust in God, can cause things in the natural realm to change. I wanted to believe God at such a level that lives and circumstances would be changed for His glory.

As I prayed, these words rose up in my heart and mind: "You have had mountain-moving faith." And then I heard the name "Ivy." Bit by bit, God revealed to me how our faith in His promise to give us our daughter made her "suddenly appear." It wasn't just by chance that she became available while we were in Russia. No, our faith actually moved the mountain that was preventing us from having a little girl. Our determination to believe God against all odds is what brought her into our lives.

For months we had been told by our Austin agency and by the Russian agency that there were no little girls available for adoption, but we refused to believe what we heard. Personally, I knew that God had placed a little girl on my heart, and that He had radically changed Tim's heart to adopt two children. I also knew that He had miraculously provided for Denis to be our son and had perfectly arranged the timing of our adoption in connection with my surgeries. God was able to do anything, I was certain of it. So I knew our little girl was there, too.

I am so thankful that Tim and I kept the faith. Because of our faith, many lives have been forever changed. Through this experience, I have learned the truth that God can do anything if we just believe. Nothing is impossible for Him.

Are you waiting for your promise to come to fruition? Don't lose hope. Your faith may be the very thing that causes that promise to suddenly appear!

CHAPTER 13

A THREE-RING CIRCUS AND A MOTOR HOME

The Holy Spirit helps us in our weakness.
ROMANS 8:26

With this exciting change in our life came many challenges—or should I say, opportunities—for God to show Himself faithful in our lives once again. Take a moment to picture this scene with me, and I think you will begin to appreciate what our family was experiencing.

Overnight, our family was enlarged by two children who didn't speak any English and who had experienced very little in life. Dalton, or Curious George as I quickly named him, was into everything. He was constantly taking things apart to see how they worked.

Due to Ivy's isolated upbringing and her reliance on her own will to survive, she had a difficult time submitting to authority. To put it mildly, she wanted what she wanted, and she wanted it when she wanted it. I spent many hours setting boundaries for her, boundaries that were backed by love. Fortunately, over time she began to let down her guard and relax.

But what surprised me the most was Ty's reaction to the children. He had been so excited about having siblings, but now that they were actually here, he wasn't so sure. Our seven-year-old son's world was suddenly invaded by two children who not only took his toys and wore his old clothes, they also took his parents. Ty didn't quite know how to handle the emotions that were going on inside of him. Nor did we. Our sweet, happy, gentle child was becoming angry, aggressive, and fighting for our attention.

To top off all this stress, I was coming off a year of invasive surgeries and transitioning from being a professional athlete to being retired from the sport that had been my life. I was still trying to accept the fact that my days of being "Kristi the skier" were gone. Throw the never-ending planning of ministry events on top of this, and all I can say is, "Poor Tim!"

Our house was like a three-ring circus. On the outside, we looked like we had it all together, but boy, within those walls, things were often chaotic and overwhelming to say the least. Again I had to learn to lay my need to control everything aside and just trust that God knew what He was doing. He had brought this family together, and He would help us through our transition.

We decided to continue our previous lifestyle as much as possible. We packed up as we'd always done and headed to water-ski and ministry events, and even moved to North Carolina for the summer. Due to the wanderings and curiosity of the children, we decided it was best if we lived in our motor home for the summer, as I wanted to maintain some consistency. I also wanted to keep the children confined to a small space so I could keep my eye on them.

One evening while in the motor home, something amazing happened. My brother Michael had noticed that I needed a break. He called and offered to have Ty for a sleepover. Ty was excited about staying at Uncle Michael's house and headed out the door of that motor home without even one backward look!

Due to commitments, Tim had remained in Florida, so it was just me and the two little Russian chatterboxes. They lay on the pulled-out sofa bed, talking excitedly about who knows what, and I just had to smile. They were so beautiful. And Ty was so beautiful. I was blessed—I knew it—but at the same time, I was so tired. I gave the kids a big hug, tucked them in for the night, then went to the back of the motor home and collapsed on the bed.

"Oh Lord," I cried out, "help me! Please give me the strength and wisdom to meet the needs of these children. And please help Ty. I know he's hurting, and I don't know how to help my baby."

At that point I realized that I didn't even know how I should pray—I didn't know what any of my children needed; none of them could communicate their hearts to me. I felt so helpless. As I poured my heart out to God, Romans 8:26–28 rose up in my spirit.

> And the Holy Spirit helps us in our weakness. For example, we don't know what God wants us to pray for. But the Holy Spirit prays for us with groanings that cannot be expressed in words. And the Father who knows all hearts knows what the Spirit is saying, for the Spirit pleads for us believers in harmony with God's own will. And we know that God causes everything to work together for the good of those who love God and are called according to his purpose for them.

I reminded God of these verses. I reminded Him that I was His child and that His Spirit resided within me. I reminded Him of His promise to intercede on my behalf before the throne of God.

"Lord, you know what I need," I began. "You know what to pray for. I ask you to pray on my behalf."

All of a sudden, my lips started moving, and I began praying in words I had never spoken before. Beautiful languages flowed from my lips, incredible songs as well. For over an hour, I sat in the back of that motor home, worshipping God and praising Him with words and songs that came from a place deep within me, a place I hadn't even know existed.

When this time came to an end, I just sat in silence in the back of my motor home. Nothing like this had ever happened to me. You would think an experience like this would have freaked me out, but it didn't. In fact, I was at complete peace and filled with joy.

Without a doubt, I knew God had heard and answered my prayers. I knew that out of His great love for me, He had interceded on my behalf and caused something to happen in the heavenly realm. With a smile on my face, I rolled over and went to sleep.

The next morning as I was reflecting on this experience, my mother knocked on the door (we were parked in their driveway) and said, "Your friend, Jo Ann, came by and dropped off this book for you this morning." The book my friend had felt moved to bring me—totally unaware of my experience the night before—was entitled, *The Holy Spirit and His Gifts*, by Kenneth E. Haggin.

The book contained a study on the power of the Holy Spirit and the individual gifts the Spirit imparts to believers. Inside these pages, I discovered an explanation of what had happened to me the night before.

I wasn't sure if I should tell anyone. What if someone thought I was crazy? What if they didn't believe me? To this day, until this writing, I have only told a few of my closest friends. This experience went against everything that I had ever learned. Unknown tongues and the world of miracles simply weren't taught in the churches I had attended, nor in the one I currently attended. Yet I couldn't deny what I had experienced or the peace I had felt. I couldn't deny that, at my time of need, God had thundered down from Heaven and met me right in the back of that motor home (Psalm 18).

After this experience, I began to seek more of God. And the more I sought of Him, the more He began to teach me about Himself. I learned very quickly that I had been putting God in a box my whole life...a nice, clean, religious box.

When I decided to let Him out of the box, He began to move in my life in new and amazing ways. The more I sought Him, the more I found Him. I began to witness unexplainable miracles in people's lives and our ministry. I also began to witness the hearts of our children being healed one by one, and my own as well. I am so thankful for God's gifts of the Spirit. It has been His Spirit that has consistently given me the strength, ability, wisdom, power, and peace to move forward through every obstacle of life.

SOMETHING TO THINK ABOUT

Until this supernatural encounter with God, I had been totally ignorant of many things of the Lord, especially the gifts of the Holy Spirit that are taught in 1 Corinthians 12—gifts such as healing, prophesying, speaking in tongues, interpretation, and miraculous powers. Yes, I had heard of them, but weren't people engaged in these activities weird, out of God's will, under the influence of Satan, or just "out there"?

Yet when I laid aside my own judgments and my years of denominational teachings and opened my heart to God to learn, He began to reveal these hidden things. When I cried out in desperation, "Lord, teach me. Reveal Yourself to me. Take me past my current understanding," He did. And as God led me into these new spiritual territories, He was faithful to bring people into my life who had knowledge of these things so that I could grow in them. God is so wonderful. He has never left me confused and alone.

More than anything, I encourage you to seek the Lord for yourself. Yes, get in a Bible-teaching church, surround yourself with godly people, go to Bible studies—these are all incredible ways to build your faith and knowledge of the Word. They are all extremely important to your spiritual growth. But do not just take everything you are taught at face value. Test what you hear. Read the Word of God for yourself. Study the context of the scriptures. Learn about the history, customs, and traditions of that time. Read commentaries.

Most importantly, inquire of the Holy Spirit. Ask Him to teach you and guide you into all truth. 1 Corinthians 2:10–12 says,

> But it was to us that God revealed these things by His Spirit. For His Spirit searches out everything and shows us God's deep secrets. No one can know a person's thoughts except that person's own spirit, and no one can know God's thoughts except

God's own Spirit. And we have received God's Spirit (not the world's spirit), so we can know the wonderful things God has freely given us.

Without a doubt, the Spirit of God is the best Source. He is willing and ready to reveal His hidden truths to His children.

Be willing to get out of your religious box. Be open to the fact that there are many things of the Lord you haven't experienced or understood. None of us knows it all. Don't base your beliefs solely on what you've been taught by others. Get into the Word yourself and ask the Holy Spirit to lead you. And finally, please, be careful not to judge people, denominations, or gifts of the Spirit based on your limited exposure or bad experiences. Yes, there are some who have abused these gifts, but don't let those people keep you from moving out into the deeper things of God.

CHAPTER 14

A CALL TO FREEDOM

I am the Lord your God, who brought you out of the
land of Egypt so you would no longer be their slaves.
I broke the yoke of slavery from your neck so you can
walk with your heads held high.
LEVITICUS 26:13

Walking away from something that had been such a huge part of my life wasn't an easy task emotionally. I was quite content as a wife, mother of three beautiful children, and leader of a growing ministry. But a part of me still yearned to be back on the water, even years after I had officially retired. This desire didn't stem from a need for more victories. I had trophies coming out the wazoo. It originated from a longing to be back in the circle of athletes.

As a noncompetitor, I felt like an outsider. I attended events and watched the athletes hanging out in their private areas, being interviewed for victories and introduced in opening ceremonies, and thought my heart might break. I felt like I was *less than* what I used to be.

From 2003, my first year off the water, until 2007, I fought these emotions, continually pushing them deeper and deeper inside of me until one day, I didn't feel them anymore. "Praise God," I thought. "I'm over it! My self-worth isn't based on being a skier anymore. I'm free!" I would soon learn otherwise.

In the summer of 2007, an inexplicable desire began stirring in my heart to compete again. This desire would rise up suddenly when I least expected it, and linger. During the night, I'd even wake up thinking about competing—specifically in the World Championship in Austria—an event that, by that time, was mere weeks away.

To compete in this event would be insane, at least that's what my husband told me. I could count the number of ski sets I had taken in the past several years on one hand. I could count on the other hand the number of workouts I'd had in the gym. My competitors, on the other hand, had been training for years for this one event, each with a single goal—to win. Going to ski in front of my peers after a four-year layoff and very little practice was not my idea of fun. I did have some dignity.

Yet the closer the event became, the stronger the desire in my heart grew to take to the water one more time. I began to sense that competing was something God was placing on my heart to do. Why? I didn't know. It didn't make sense to me or to anyone else. Yet, I couldn't deny its powerful presence.

With less than two weeks to prepare for the World Championships, I started training and making arrangements for my trip. Since my time on the water was limited, I had to make every set count.

My mind focused intently on the task at hand, quickly bringing up mental images and sending them forth to my body. Fortunately, my body, although throbbing with pain, responded to my mind's direction. I actually skied surprisingly well during those two weeks of preparation, consistently posting scores that would be high enough to win the event. I was also pleasantly surprised to discover that my hips didn't hurt while I was skiing. I hadn't taken my new hips for a test drive since that total pelvic reconstruction in 2004, so this was exciting.

With every pass, my confidence began to rise. Could God really be leading me back to the water after a four-year retirement for a gold medal—a medal that would bring glory to His name and an opportunity to build a stronger platform for the ministry? I had just read world boxing champion George Foreman's memoir, *God in My Corner*. Surely God was going to bring me back to the top of the podium once again, just like He did for Big George. Maybe I'd even have my own commercials and line of appliances!

But this adventure wouldn't be the journey to gold I was hoping for. Rather, it was to be a journey to finding freedom from things that were still holding me captive, so that I could find real victory and finally realize my true worth.

Looking back, I have to laugh. I had been so sure that I was completely free from determining my own identity by my performance on the water; free from trying to "be" someone; free of being afraid of what people thought of me. But I wasn't free at all—I just hadn't been in a place where those things could rise up and expose their ugly heads.

On August 26, Ty and I arrived in Linz, Austria, at the 2007 World Championships. Two days after arriving, I found myself standing on the starting dock with skiers from all over the world who were likely wondering the same thing I was: *What in the world is* she *doing here?*

When my turn came, I tuned out everything around me to the best of my ability and slipped into the water, ready to give it my all. My first pass was amazing. I felt strong, in rhythm, and at peace. I breathed a huge sigh of relief when I dropped into the water for the boat judge to shorten the rope for my next run.

My second pass, still a warm-up, started very smoothly. Around the third buoy, however, my left hip gave way. I tried desperately to stay in the game, quickly turning buoy number four, knowing that if I just remained calm, I could make it to the end of the pass and regroup. Yet when I went to turn the fifth buoy, my hip collapsed again. I was done. I let go of the rope and skied toward the far side of the lake, away from the crowd, and tried to gather my emotions.

I was in complete shock. This was an opener pass for me, a mere warm-up. How could this have happened?

A myriad of questions flowed through my mind, "Why God? Why call me back to the water? Why make me go through all the physical pain to prepare for this trip? Why allow me to ski so well in practice and get my hopes up for a victory only to let me fall flat on my face?"

I am embarrassed to admit it, but I was angry. For the first time in my life, I was openly angry at God. Pride rose up in me that I didn't even know existed. Finally the words, *"How could You do this to me?"* erupted from my mouth. In my heart of hearts, I felt like God Himself had deliberately led me to the slaughter.

With those words, my emotions changed from being in shock over my performance to being in shock over my words! I sat in the water with tears running down my cheeks as I cried out, "I'm so sorry, God."

That moment in time revealed a not-so-pretty side of myself, a side oozing with pride, frustration, irritation, anger, fear, and embarrassment. I could only imagine what people were saying about me on the shoreline and in the water-ski chat rooms online. I was utterly humiliated and over-whelmingly frustrated.

More than anything, I had wanted to give God glory in my perfor-mance. I wanted the world to see what He could do. I wanted everyone to know that with Him, all things were possible.

As I look back at this situation, however, I now see a common theme. Although I wanted God to receive glory in this journey, I wanted it to come in a way that was pleasing to my flesh—like a successful run on the water, ending with a gold medal hanging around my neck! Little did I know this journey wasn't about me pointing people to Him through my skiing; rather, it was about my skiing pointing out areas of my life that needed some fine-tuning.

In the middle of a cold lake in Austria, God began a work of free-dom in my life. Over the next two years, this work would continue on the water as I continued to compete at selected events. Try as I might, though, my skiing performance failed to reach my preretirement level. In fact, I didn't even make it through to a finals round. It was a humbling experience.

But as I continued the competitions, I began to realize that, for the first time in a very long time, I was actually enjoying the ride. For so long, I had been under so much pressure to perform at a certain level that I had missed the beauty of the journey. Now, in the midst of this new journey, I finally got it.

I finally got the fact that skiing was a gift from God, one that was meant to be enjoyed and to be used for His glory. I finally accepted that my worth wasn't determined by the scores I posted. I finally understood that God loved me whether I ever stood on a podium or not. I also acknowledged that God never leads His children to slaughter, as I had first thought. I found instead that He consistently guides His children to victory.

It's just that our victory often comes in ways we don't expect.

The truth is, God loves us so much that He allows us to go through situations that He knows have the potential to move us to the next level in our faith—to the top of God's podium, you might say. He brings us through experiences that have the potential to purify us and make us more like Him so that we can experience the incredible life that He died to give us…a life of peace and joy. A life of freedom!

By the end of 2009, my skiing had improved dramatically. Once again I was posting scores in competitions that had the potential for victory. But it didn't last long. During the final competition of that year, as I rounded the fifth buoy of my run, I injured my left knee. After surgery and rehab, the desire to ski was gone. Just as quickly as it had risen in my heart for the World Championships in 2007, it now disappeared. And I was okay with that. There were other things dear to my heart now—new dreams and desires. I no longer felt the need to be "Kristi, the skier." I no longer felt empty or worthless without a title tied to my name or unaccepted because I wasn't one of *them* anymore. I was finally free—free to move forward to what God had next.

SOMETHING TO THINK ABOUT

Many times in life, God places ideas and dreams in our hearts that make absolutely no sense to anyone. In man's opinion (and in my own reasoning), returning to the water after a four-year absence was ludicrous. Yet I knew in the depths of my heart it was something the Lord wanted me to do.

How did I know this? I'm glad you asked.

First of all, the idea to compete continually rose up in my heart. No matter how hard I tried to reason it away, it remained. Furthermore, I was certain that this wasn't a crazy Kristi idea. Competing again wasn't something my flesh actively wanted to do. I had become quite happy in my new life being a mom to my three amazing children and ministering to people across the nation and even the world. But somehow, deep within, I just *knew* that competing in Austria was something I was supposed to do.

Only now, as I look back years later, can I see some of the reasons behind what seemed to be God's madness. With my 20/20 hindsight, I now know God used that time to bring healing to my heart. He completed a work in me that I was unaware needed to be done, but He also used that time to develop relationships with a new generation of athletes from around the world—athletes I've now been able to minister to and even mentor that I might not have connected with otherwise.

Is God leading you to do something strange, something you or no one else understands? Is there a desire burning in your heart that simply won't go away no matter how hard you try to suppress it? Perhaps it's time to lay aside your questions, pride, and fear, and simply step out in faith. You may not understand the ways of God, but you can trust His heart. Whatever He asks you to do will be backed by His love, grace, power, and provision. Who knows, freedom just might be waiting for you, too!

CHAPTER 15

FAITH IN ACTION

*What good is it, dear brothers and sisters, if you say you have
faith but don't show it by your actions?*

JAMES 2:14

With my newfound freedom, I finally had the peace I needed to move forward into the next chapter of life. No longer did I feel a tug in my heart to go back to the water; it was time for a new thing. It was time to take all the Lord had blessed me with—my experiences, accolades, resources, and talents—and use them wholeheartedly for His glory.

It had been seven years since In His Wakes had launched out into the deep with God. During that time, God had brought together an incredible team with a heart and passion to serve Him, including a faithful director, Nate Miller. Nate and his wife, Ivy, stepped into the role of the D2R Director in 2007. Under their leadership and with the help of hundreds of volunteers, thousands of at-risk children are finding victory in Christ through the sport I love.

Now that Nate and Ivy were coordinating and hosting the D2R events, I could sense God pouring another vision into my heart. Through my involvement with IHW, I had met many people who had encountered incredible difficulties in life. God had used these children, teens, and adults to open my eyes to a world that, by the grace of God, I had never known—a world of abuse, neglect, violence, abandonment, hopelessness, poverty, and addiction.

As we raised our three children in our small community, God began to open my eyes to the truth that *this* world was all around me. It wasn't just at IHW events, it was everywhere—including Keystone Heights. This became obvious one day as I was sitting at the main intersection of our town, waiting for the light to turn green. There I witnessed a woman being pushed around by a man at a local gas station. They were in a crowded area in broad daylight, next to a line of cars waiting for the light, but no one did anything. People just stared.

Without thinking, I drove my car over the curb, opened the door, and told her to get in. She climbed into the passenger seat, and the angered man repeatedly reached into the car, attempting to snatch her purse from her hands. While he yelled threatening obscenities at us both, we somehow managed to get the door shut and drive away.

As I drove around town, trying to figure out what to do next, I began to talk with this lady. Through tears, she shared her life story. Sophia was from Poland. She had come to America for a better life. Her dreams of success, however, were quickly overshadowed by her circumstances. The man I saw hitting her was her husband. He wasn't the first who had taken a swing at her.

Sophia and her husband had come to Keystone Heights to spend the afternoon sunbathing on our city beach and swimming in our local lake. They were also there to purchase drugs. During their visit, an argument had escalated to the scene being played out before me.

For over an hour, Sophia and I sat in the car, making phone calls and trying to figure out what to do next. But there simply wasn't anywhere to take her in our remote town. No safe place to go. I called pastors, friends, agencies—anyone I could think of—to no avail.

Out of options, I ended up taking her to our home, where she stayed with us until late in the evening. We took that time to love on her, feed her, encourage her, and pray with her. She even went water-skiing and flew in Tim's plane. Yet in the end, unable to see a way out of her situation, she asked to be taken back to her home in Gainesville. We never saw or heard from her again.

Our experience with Sophia pierced our family's heart. There was no denying the bruises on her body or the fear and hopelessness in her eyes. There was also no denying the sense of frustration I felt over the lack of local help and my own inability to bring change to her life.

God soon began to bring other people my way—people struggling with lifelong addictions, homelessness, poverty, domestic violence, and mental illness, among other things. He was revealing to me, once again, the incredible need for the Lord and real tangible help in the lives of people in our community. I sensed the Lord saying, "I have shown you a need; now fill it."

I began to earnestly pray about what the Lord would have me do. I felt a stirring to create another nonprofit organization called Kristi Overton Johnson Ministries (KOJM). The mission of KOJM is to encourage hearts, equip minds, and evangelize the gospel of Jesus Christ. This organization would establish a local resource center called Champion's Heart, in order to help people who, like Sophia, found themselves overwhelmed by hardship.

Champion's Heart would offer help and hope to local residents. Since Keystone Heights is located at the intersection of four counties, and most help agencies are many miles away in the heart of each county, there was a great need for a facility where established agencies could offer services to our community. Champion's Heart would be that place. It would also be a place where Christians could fulfill the ministries the Lord had placed on their hearts.

God provided a beautiful facility to carry out this vision. One day while I was walking through our community during my morning exercise routine, I came upon what had once been St. Anne's Episcopal Church. As I passed, I heard the words, "This is your building."

I stopped and began to look around the facility. It spanned over a city block, complete with a fellowship hall, office complex, and chapel.

Amazingly, somehow in the fifteen years I had lived in Keystone Heights, I had failed to notice it.

Upon returning home, I made some calls and discovered that the building was under contract to be sold. I wasn't too concerned. Through my previous experiences with the Lord, I knew God would make a way for me to have that building if it was indeed His will. As I hung up the phone, I placed the building in God's hands.

Many months passed, and the building just sat there. In May of 2010, I decided to inquire once again about the building. Just as before, I was told that the building was under contract and was to close the very next week.

"God, if this is what You desire, please make a way," I prayed.

I went on about my business, preparing for upcoming events and spending time with my kids. Just as we were about to leave for the summer to go to North Carolina, I received a call from my realtor, Sue Plaster.

"Kristi, have you left for the Carolinas yet?" she asked excitedly.

"No," I answered. "I leave in a couple of days. I'm in St. Petersburg (Florida) with my kids, spending time with Tim's family."

"Well, get back in town!" she exclaimed. "I just rode by St. Anne's, and there's a huge for sale sign on the property. The contract that was on the buildings fell through!"

I hightailed it back to Keystone, took a tour of the facilities, and on June 13, 2010, made an offer. Within two weeks, we owned the facility. Once again, God had proven Himself faithful.

That fall, Champion's Heart opened its doors. Since then, with the help of many people on the ministry team, various organizations began to make Champion's Heart Life Center their new home. In addition, relationships with over a hundred help agencies were developed, offering residents in our community direct access to much needed resources. Several ministries were launched on our property as well. Praise God, hundreds of people have found hope and help to enable them to break free of bondage and move forward victoriously at Champion's Heart.

Not long after we were in the center, I felt a stirring in my heart to publish a magazine called *Victorious Living*. At first I thought this publication was to be a local resource magazine providing information about events and opportunities in our town. With this focus, the first issue was published in August 2011. It didn't take long, however, for the Lord to show me that this magazine was not purposed to be a resource magazine. Instead, it was to be a publication testifying to the faithful provision of my God. I would soon get a glimpse of the great plans He had in store for *Victorious Living*.

With the visions of all these ministries stirring in my heart and mind, I set out doing the only thing I knew to do—work hard, work long, and press through every trial that rose up against me. These traits had helped me become a world champion athlete; surely they were what were needed to make these ministries a success.

Not exactly.

SOMETHING TO THINK ABOUT

When God answered my prayers and put the keys of the Champion's Heart facility in my hands, I must confess, I was overwhelmed. What had only been a dream, a mere vision, was now a reality. One glance at all the things that needed to be remodeled was enough to make my head spin!

"How in the world am I going to do all of this?" I thought.

Seeing my anxiety, Ron, a gentleman who had come on the ministry staff to help me establish the center and raise funding said, "Kristi, don't look at all that has to be done. We are going to pick one thing, a manageable thing, and get started. Tomorrow, we paint the hallway."

Ron had a plan. We were going to paint the hallway, then the offices, kitchen, and fellowship hall. After those things were accomplished, we would remodel the chapel and then make our way across the street to yet another office complex.

Each day we focused on the task at hand. And you know what? Everything that needed to get done, got done. Within a week, the doors of Champion's Heart were open and able to begin ministering to people. And within five months after taking possession, the facilities were completely remodeled, and a grand opening was held.

Ron's wise words have helped me on many occasions to realign my thinking and put things in proper perspective.

Is there a task you have been given that seems too great? Have you found yourself paralyzed with fear, wondering where in the world you should even start? Take Ron's advice. Find yourself a *hallway* and get started. Little by little, you will see your vision come to reality.

CHAPTER 16

FULL SPEED AHEAD

Be well balanced, be vigilant and cautious
at all times; for that enemy of yours,
the devil, roams around like a lion roaring,
seeking someone to seize upon and devour.
1 PETER 5:8

With the ministries of In His Wakes expanding, *Victorious Living* launched, and Champion's Heart growing, I found myself excited beyond words. I love being a part of what God is doing. I enjoy challenging, God-sized projects and stepping out in faith to accomplish them. It's just how I'm wired.

Two of my greatest strengths are my creative mind and my persevering spirit. God has given me the ever-churning mind of a visionary and the passionate determination to see His visions through. These strengths have been useful in becoming a champion on water skis as well as for pioneering ministries. They've also helped me overcome adversity. But these same traits, when left unattended and unbridled, have at times created problems.

In a flash, I can be off chasing after with unending determination what seems to be an incredible idea, only to find myself running in circles—as we say in the South, like a chicken with its head cut off! On many occasions, my passionate spirit has led me down paths God probably didn't intend for me to travel. It's not that those paths were necessarily bad. In fact, many of them were good, and they touched many lives. But they weren't always God's best for my life. If there's one thing I've learned, it's

117

that there is a *huge* difference between a good idea and a God-idea. God-ideas are certainly the way to go!

When I received the visions of IHW, Champion's Heart, and *Victorious Living,* I set sail. And boy, did I set sail.

The problem, however, was that I didn't have my sail up all the time so God could lead me where He wanted me to go. Instead, I chased after ideas with every ounce of energy I could muster. In my defense, with every chasing, my heart was pure. I loved the Lord. I wanted to serve Him, and I wanted to help people. God had placed huge visions on my heart, and more than anything, I wanted to make Him proud by making them a success. But just because my intentions were good didn't mean that my actions were always right.

Undoubtedly, I made mistakes as I threw myself 100 percent into serving God and others. In my quest, I often overlooked what God truly wanted from me...a relationship with Him based on trust and love, and a relationship with those He had placed in my path. The ugly truth is that many times I got so busy doing for God that I often missed being with Him and the precious people in front of me. This led to much exhaustion, frustration, anxiety, and physical sickness for the first ten years of my ministry journey.

As an athlete, I know all too well the principle that anything out of balance falls. But at times I have overlooked this principle in ministry. I learned the hard way that when you don't take time to rest, eat right, or exercise; when you work yourself around the clock and ignore relationships that bring joy into your life; and when you ignore the instructions of the Lord, you get out of balance, and you fall.

After observing my quest from the sidelines, my husband lovingly said to me one day, "Kristi, for years I witnessed you successfully balance your water-ski career with college and even law school. You balanced relationships and took time for your friends, family, and yourself. But since you entered into ministry, you are one of the most unbalanced people I know!"

Although the words weren't fun to hear, I knew in my heart that Tim was right. Did I mention that at the time he spoke these words, I was curled up in a fetal position in the middle of my closet, sobbing uncontrollably? Not exactly a picture of victory.

I can say with certainty that I was not in balance at that point of my life. I worked physically and processed mentally from early morning till late at night. I ceased exercising, and unfortunately, failed to nurture precious relationships.

I had fallen into the trap of a wrong belief pattern—the idea that I needed to work nonstop for God to make the ministries He had placed on my heart a success. God had, after all, called me to do something special for His kingdom. Talk about pressure!

I can remember on several occasions my children coming into my office and asking me to play with them. My answer? "In a little while. Mommy is helping people. Go watch television."

I justified my constant answering of emails, returning phone calls, and sharing the mission of our ministry as being more important than being with my kids. I was, after all, helping underprivileged children.

I also allowed my relationship with my husband to get out of balance. Night after night, Tim would call out to me from our bedroom, "You coming to bed?"

"I'll be there soon; just let me finish a few emails," was my usual response.

I found it so difficult to pull myself away from the computer. There was work to do, lives to save, events to organize, and sponsorships to secure. Minutes turned into hours as I worked into the wee hours of the morning, trying to get one more thing done—all the while ignoring Tim's needs and his simple desire to curl up with his wife and go to sleep. And it was something I needed desperately, as well.

I felt such internal pressure to succeed—greater even than what I had experienced on the water as a world champion athlete. Every day, voices from within told me I needed to do more for God in order to please Him. And I believed those voices.

One day as I sat at the end of the dock, looking over the water and stressing over my never-ending to-do-for-God list, I asked, "Lord, why is accomplishing what You have called me to do so hard?"

Immediately, I saw a mental picture of myself. There I was, sitting on the edge of the boat with one leg in the driver's seat and the other leg dangling in the water with my ski attached to my foot. I was trying to drive the boat and ski at the same time. It was quite a comical picture. My first thought was, "That sure isn't going to work!"

Even a world champion skier is limited in her abilities if she refuses to get behind the boat. Sure, I may be able to ski straight down the lake with one leg hanging out of the boat, but what fun is that? There's no way I could run the course, cut back and forth on the ski, or be victorious, unless I chose to let go of the controls and get behind the boat.

Through that mental picture, God showed me the reality that the reason I was so exhausted and struggling to move forward was because I was in essence trying to ski and drive simultaneously. I was trying to hold on to the controls and direct my life and ministry instead of trusting God to lead.

On my dock, God lovingly showed me that He didn't need me to be a superwomen to carry out His plans. He didn't need me to make things happen or beg and manipulate people to help me achieve my God-given goals. He simply needed me to get behind the boat—follow His lead, take steps of obedience, and trust Him by faith to provide.

I wish I could say that after receiving this revelation, I immediately jumped behind the boat and said, "Hit it, God! I'm following You. Take me wherever You want to go, and take as long as You'd like."

But I didn't. Not even close.

For years, I continued to push my mind and body to the limits. As IHW grew and Champion's Heart was being founded, I took on more and more responsibility without ever considering the effect it would have on my home life and my physical, mental, and emotional health. I also allowed, without godly discernment, numerous people complete access into my life. Carelessly, I revealed my innermost thoughts and secrets and gave away my precious time and energy—things that should have been reserved for my loved ones. The end result was physical sickness that impacted not only my life, but our entire family.

One by one, symptoms began to manifest in my body—all-over body pain, stiffness, burning sensations in my muscles, itching under my skin, constant pressure and spinning in my head, fainting spells, memory loss, fatigue, chronic stomach pain, bloating, intestinal blockages followed by intestinal explosions, overactive bladder, bouts of anxiety, and abnormal heart palpitations.

Over a period of ten years, I spent tens of thousands of dollars and countless hours, searching for medical explanations for my physical conditions. Over and over again I heard, "You are the healthiest sick person I've ever met," as each doctor shook his head, puzzled by my condition.

When the medical world failed to have answers, I sought the advice of nutritionists and other alternative medical approaches. I sought spiritual help, too. I prayed. I fasted. I searched the scriptures and spoke God's Word over my life. I repented of any known sin. I tried everything and visited anyone who had the potential of helping me feel better.

Ultimately, I was diagnosed with Lyme disease and fibromyalgia, two chronic diseases that are greatly impacted by stress. The more I researched those diseases and listened to the experts, however, the more hopeless I began to feel.

"Lord," I cried out in desperation, "I know You've called me to these ministries. I know You've called me to be a wife to Tim and mother to these three amazing children. But how can I fulfill Your call when I feel like this? I can't finish a sentence without my brain wandering off. I can't go twenty minutes without going to the bathroom. I can hardly eat without my stomach becoming obstructed. I'm passing out walking through the house. My head is spinning out of control, and I'm exhausted. Not to mention, emotionally, I feel like a time bomb just waiting to explode. Please God, help me. Help me get out of this pit!"

I truly felt like I was in a pit and no matter how hard I tried to get out of it, I just kept sliding back down. Only my husband and children know how terribly sick I was for so long.

To keep from falling into despair, I made some conscious choices. First of all, I determined to focus more on God, the true Giver of life, than on the symptoms, diagnosis, and prognosis. With all the information circulating on the web and the negative testimonies of others, it would have been very easy to believe the lie that I would never get well.

Second, I chose to focus on the Lord and His love for me. He cared about what I was going through, and His love would lead me to victory. Third, I remembered the visions God had placed in my heart and the promises He's given in His Word, and I stood on them, even when they seemed far from being fulfilled. God is faithful. If He placed these dreams in my heart, then I knew He would faithfully bring them to fruition. Finally, I chose to step out in faith and push myself beyond my feelings.

During this period of my life, there were days that I didn't feel like getting out of bed, much less ministering God's hope and love to others. Yet as I chose to rise up, step forward in faith, and prayerfully follow God's leading, He powerfully infused me with His incredible strength and enabled me to use my gifts for His glory. More times than not, during those times of ministering, my symptoms miraculously disappeared. It's an amazing phenomenon.

God's strength is the most amazing thing I have ever experienced. It literally transforms me from the inside out, giving me supernatural power that enables me to do things that would be impossible if I was depending on myself. Serving others has definitely been the best medicine for my health!

Praise God, complete healing did finally manifested in my body and mind—but it took years. Unlike some people who are healed miraculously in an instant, my healing came over time. And you know what? I'm thankful for that journey. I'm thankful God didn't just poof away my problems. I'm thankful that He loved me enough to expose the root of my issues so that I could escape their grasp.

My symptoms are what kept me close to the Lord. My symptoms caused me to experience the strength of God in the midst of my weakness, and they showed me the difference of relying on Him instead of my own strength.

Because I know myself so well, I am certain that if God had chosen to instantly make me well, I would have moved through life at double the speed. I would have run faster and faster for Him, all the while running further and further away from Him and my family.

SOMETHING TO THINK ABOUT

I want to take a moment to encourage anyone who endures daily chronic pain and illnesses. My heart goes out to you. I know from experience how overwhelming and discouraging it can be. If that's you, don't give up. Don't lose hope! "'I know the plans I have for you,' says the LORD. 'They are plans for good and not for disaster, to give you a future and a hope'" (Jeremiah 29:11).

God has a plan. I know it's hard to understand His plan sometimes, especially in the midst of chronic physical pain. But don't let your circumstances or how you feel cause you to doubt God's love and will for your life. More than anything, He desires for you to experience a life of health and wholeness. He died to give it to you! (John 10:10; 3 John 1:2; Isaiah 53:4–5)

Stand on the Word. Stand on His promises and trust the very heart and nature of God. He has not forgotten you. He sees you right where you are, and He is right there in the middle of it all, upholding and sustaining you with His unfathomable love and grace.

I know it isn't easy, but keep pressing forward one day at a time, one step at a time if need be. One way to advance is through praise. Praising God changes everything. It broke the chains off Peter and Silas, and it will break the chains off you (Acts 16:25–26).

Go ahead—praise Him right now, in the midst of your trial. Give thanks for the health you do have and thank Him in advance for the healing He has already provided at the cross. Don't let your circumstances, doubts, or the enemy steal what is rightfully yours.

As you wait for your healing to manifest in your body, rest in the truth that God can use you right now, right where you are. During my more than ten years of chronic physical trials and the inconveniences of over a dozen surgeries, God was still at work in my life, teaching me, loving me, using me, and bringing me ever closer to Him. Not one moment, not one pain, and not one tear was ever wasted.

As I've been willing, God has taken me by the hand, lifted me up, and carried me along—all the while giving me supernatural strength to accomplish the things He has called me to do, things that should have been impossible given my physical situation. He will do the same for you.

Remember, with God nothing is impossible. Whether you are healthy as a horse or lying flat on your back, God can still use your life to touch the lives of many. Trust Him and begin to praise Him right now for your victory. It's on the way.

CHAPTER 17

DISCOVERING TRUTH

*They traded the truth about God for a lie. So they worshiped
and served the things God created instead of the Creator
himself, who is worthy of eternal praise! Amen.*

ROMANS 1:25

When I consider my journey to health, I realize that my physical health arrived through my being willing to cooperate with the Lord. I needed to give God complete access to my heart and mind and then follow His lead to bring about much needed change. I didn't just have symptoms that needed to be eliminated. There were thought processes, lifestyle choices, stressors, attitudes, words, and relationships that needed attention.

Making changes in my thought-life and lifestyle was difficult. My mind and body had run at full speed in one direction for so long, it was like my life's accelerator was stuck in that position! My natural reaction was to think negatively and to commit to people and activities, to push my physical body beyond its limits, and to work nonstop.

Radical changes were in order if I was going to break free of what had become a destructive cycle of thoughts and performance in my life. I couldn't continue in my current pattern if I wanted to experience the fullness of God's blessings in my life—mainly health.

First on the change list? My mind.

Thus far, I haven't really shared with you the mental and emotional struggles I've experienced, either on the water as an athlete or on the shore as a wife, mother, daughter, friend, and ministry leader. For years, deep within my spirit, I constantly struggled with misplaced worth and identity, a fear of disappointing people or looking foolish, and a fear of failing and falling. Truthfully, anger and self-hate had brewed in my heart for years.

As I sit here pondering whether I should share more, I'm torn. Part of me wants to skip right over this part of my story, to erase it and protect my parents from having to read about the private emotional battle their daughter engaged in for years. Yet I can't quite seem to get my finger to press the delete button, because I know that eliminating this chapter would eliminate a big part of my story. Eliminating this chapter could also very well prevent someone else from finding true freedom and joy. So here goes, complete access to my heart and mind...

It is quite clear to me that the biggest battle I've ever faced was the ongoing battle between my ears. If given the opportunity to peek inside my mind during the 80s, 90s, and early 2000s, one would be absolutely amazed (or even shocked) at the thoughts that plagued my inner being on a daily basis.

When I think about my childhood, it's hard to imagine how these thoughts could have ever taken root. Unlike so many people I have met in my many years of ministering, I was blessed with the love of two amazing parents who supported me then and continue to support me now in every way. Within the walls of my home, I was protected and shielded from the evils of the world. I was spared the horrors so many people go through—abuse, addictive behaviors, domestic turmoil, belittlement by harsh words.

My parents loved me as God intends parents to love their children. I felt safe, special, and able to do anything. One of my favorite memories as a child is my father telling me good night. Every evening, he would enter my room singing the theme song from the Miss America beauty pageant at the top of his lungs, "T-H-E-R-E she is, M-I-S-S America!" Then he'd kneel down by my bed and proceed to tell me the story of how little Kristi would become the best skier in the whole world.

Yet even in the midst of what appeared to be a perfect environment, my self-image and sense of self-worth became dangerously twisted. It began in my early teenage years, when little by little I started believing what I now know were lies straight from Satan himself—lies that convinced me that I needed to perform at a certain level to be loved and accepted; lies that suggested I needed to act, look, and even talk a particular way to please those around me, even God.

The older I became, the more I bought into these lies, and ultimately, the more I pushed myself to do more and perform at a higher standard in every area of my life—skiing, academics, relationships, ministry, and home life. Although this concept made for a clean house, great grades, and many accolades, it unfortunately left me with a sense of never being good enough. It pushed me harder than my body was designed to go. It caused me to mentally process beyond what is healthy. It also left me physically sick, literally doubled over in pain for a large portion of my life due to incredible stomach attacks caused by self-induced stress.

One of the most helpful pieces of advice my father had given me as an athlete was to focus on beating myself, rather than trying to beat my competitors. He knew if I focused on performing to my highest level, I would finish on top. And he was right.

A problem arose, however, when I took this concept of "beating Kristi" to an unhealthy level. In my eyes, nothing I ever accomplished was good enough. Whether on the water as an athlete or on land as a daughter, wife, mother, friend, or ministry leader, there was always room for improvement. As a result, I failed to experience a sense of contentment or peace.

Because of my overwhelming drive to succeed, I was constantly judging my performance to see if there was room for improvement. Ultimately, I became my greatest critic on the water and in life. Rarely did I congratulate myself on a job well done, even when I stood on the top of the podium. I was too busy analyzing how I could have performed better.

Perfection was the goal. Little did I know—perfection wasn't possible.

I didn't realize how deeply this thought pattern of not being good enough had affected me until a few years ago when a pastor and his team began to pray over me. Minutes into his prayer, he stopped and looked at me and said, "Kristi, the Lord wants you to forgive yourself for not winning all the time. He wants you to forgive yourself for not being perfect."

Unexpectedly, I started weeping uncontrollably, overwhelmed by feelings of grief. It was like a floodgate was lifted, and years of suppressed emotions were released all at once. As the prayer continued, I was instructed to verbally forgive myself. As I said the words, "I forgive you," it was like a weight was lifted off my shoulders.

For so many years I had felt like a failure and a disappointment, even in the midst of incredible success and affirmations from my family. Through a precious young girl named Lorenza Ruiz, the Lord began to free me from this lie.

Lorenza, a native of Mexico, had come to live with us in order to improve her water-skiing skills. She quickly became a part of our family. During her time with us, we took Lorenza to many competitions. For the first time in my career, I found myself standing on the shoreline, anxiously watching someone I loved compete, someone I had spent hours training. More than anything, I wanted Lorenza to do her best—not for me, but for her! I knew how hard she had trained; I knew how well she had been skiing; and I knew how much performing well on the water would mean to her.

At one particular tournament, Lorenza fell short of her goals. After she had a moment to dry off and collect her equipment, we piled back into the car and headed home. From the backseat of the car, Lorenza whispered in her Spanish accent, "I'm so sorry I disappointed you."

I couldn't believe my ears. Disappointed me? How could she think she had let me down? I loved her. I was proud of her. I wasn't disappointed *in* her; I was disappointed *for* her. I didn't care how well she skied. I just wanted her to be happy and fulfilled.

As I looked at her reflection in the car mirror, I suddenly saw myself as a child, sitting in the backseat of my family car, heading home from an event. I could see myself, like Lorenza, filled with sadness as my parents drove home.

It was one of those *aha!* moments. I finally got it. All those years that I had sat in the back of the car, thinking that my parents were disappointed in me and my performance...it was all a lie. My parents weren't disappointed *in* me; they were disappointed *for* me. There is a huge difference between the two.

Now I sat in the front seat of the car with a sad skier in the backseat, and I finally understood. In the quiet of all those drives home, my parents hadn't been angry with me; rather, their hearts had been breaking for me. I looked at Lorenza, and I suddenly realized there are no magical words to mend a broken heart.

For years I had traded the truth for a lie. The truth was that my parents loved me. Yes, they wanted me to perform well, but my performance didn't change how they felt about me, their daughter. It didn't change how I felt about Lorenza, either.

As a young child, however, my brain didn't know how to process what was going on. During the ride home from an event, my mind reasoned the only thing that seemed logical, my parents *must* be disappointed. They had spent so much time, effort, and money on me. They had built me my own lake for goodness sakes! Surely I needed to ski well to make it all worthwhile. Unfortunately, as an adult, I carried this belief with me.

You may be asking, what's the big deal? The big deal is that the lies I believed became the foundation for my life. They were the driving force behind my words and actions. For example, I filled my life with activity and worked hard, but these actions didn't stem solely from a good work ethic. The truth is, I kept myself in motion because I never felt like I had done enough. I never felt that what I had accomplished was good enough.

These lies, once accepted as truth, impacted my life for decades. They impacted my self-worth and brought thoughts of condemnation and guilt into my heart and mind. They twisted the innocent comments that people, especially my parents, made into negative things and caused me to react defensively. They also caused me to constantly feel disappointed in myself, to the point that I didn't even like who I was.

Sadly, they have even impacted my children as each one has struggled with the notion of having to be perfect just like their mother. Through my own strivings, I unknowingly and unintentionally passed on the unspoken standard that everyone must constantly do more and perform better. It has taken years to help my children overcome this, as well as other wrong belief patterns.

It's truly amazing how early in life our thoughts can become tainted. Satan is a dirty dog. According to John 10:10, his whole purpose is to kill our dreams, steal our peace and joy, and destroy our lives. And he starts young. He knows if he can get us to grab hold of a lie that causes us to question our worth and acceptance at an early age, he will have a greater chance of sabotaging our victory as we grow older. I've seen it happen time and time again.

When we adopted our youngest two children, our oldest, biological son Ty entered into a wrestling contest with negative thoughts that could have easily led him down a path of destruction. As you can imagine, there was a lot of excitement surrounding our international adoption. Everywhere we went, people asked questions about the adoption and wanted to see the new children. Although Tim and I were extra careful to continually remind Ty how much we loved him through our words and actions, we had some tough competition. Satan was flooding his seven-year-old mind with lies that everyone loved his brother and sister more.

How freeing it was for Ty to admit those thoughts, to replace the lie with the truths that he is loved and that our love for him runs deep. Can you imagine if he had continued to build his life on the lie that we loved our other children more? He would have surely felt second best, and every action that Tim and I ever took toward the younger children would have had a perceived undertone that we loved them more. This would have created a cycle of hate and jealousy.

A lie that truly broke my heart was exposed one night when I was reading a bedtime story about a lion named Leo to our middle son, Dalton. Everywhere Leo went, people ran away because they were afraid of him. At the end of the story, Dalton looked at me and said, "Momma, I'm like Leo the lion."

I was confused and asked him to explain what he meant. Dalton responded with these words: "Nobody wanted me either." He began to explain how people would come into the orphanage and take home other children, leaving him behind. "Something was wrong with me, Momma, or they would have picked me."

I quickly looked at Dalton and responded with these words of truth, "Dalton, those people couldn't pick you because God was saving you for us!"

You should have seen the light in his eyes as he looked at me and said, "Oh! That makes perfect sense!"

Can you imagine how a lifetime of believing that something was wrong with you, that no one wanted you, would impact your life? Add to that other lies such as being stupid because of his dyslexia, that his biological mother must not have loved him, and worries that Tim and I would leave him like others had done in the past. Unless these thoughts were exposed and replaced with truth, he would have had no hope of victory.

Our daughter, too, has been in a constant battle with wrong thought patterns. Ivy grew up in a hospital in Russia where there was little food and little interaction with people. She also had been abandoned by her mother in an apartment building, and I suspect, abused by either someone in her family or a caretaker. Ivy survived because she was a fighter, and she brought this fighter mentality with her.

Since her adoption, my precious daughter and I have been on a journey to establish a foundation of truth. One by one, we've torn down lies such as "I can't trust anyone" (a lie that caused her to reject authority); "I have to protect myself" (a lie that caused her to constantly fight for her rights); and "I have to provide for myself" (a lie that kept her from accepting help and instruction from others).

As we've replaced these lies with truth through consistent actions of love and words of affirmation, this little girl, once described in a Russian courtroom as a "wild animal," has begun to be transformed into a trusting, gentle, and loving child.

Friend, I pray that through the above examples, your eyes have been opened to the importance of your thoughts. They are truly the foundation on which your life either will stand or fall. Your thoughts affect every part of your being.

SOMETHING TO THINK ABOUT

Have you ever thought about how negative thoughts, words, emotions, and self-hate must grieve our Lord? Somehow as Christians, we often feel it is acceptable, perhaps even our duty, to put ourselves down or to feel bad about ourselves. We are, after all, just lowly sinners saved by grace. We even justify our negative words and thoughts as humility, falsely assuming that the less we think of ourselves, or the more aware we are of our failures, the better Christian we will become. This couldn't be further from the truth.

For years, I put myself down, especially in the presence of others. One of my greatest fears was that someone would think that I thought more highly of myself than I ought, or that I was perfect in any way. Therefore, I spoke words of condemnation regarding my physical appearance, intelligence, or abilities in order to paint some humble picture in the minds of others. I even, at times, joined in activities that were against my moral standards to prove the point that I wasn't any different than anyone else.

Now, isn't that ironic? The very standard I sought—perfection—was the very character trait I feared someone would attribute to me. Talk about a hard battle to win.

All throughout my teenage and young adult years, I failed to consider the power of my words. The Bible says life and death are in the power of our tongue. For decades, my words were containers of death, ultimately leading me to believe the very things I spoke about myself.

When I looked in the mirror, I didn't see God's treasured possession. Instead, I saw the reflection of an ugly, fat, stupid, imperfect, forgetful person. A far cry from the person God created and saw, and a far cry from the person I actually was. Add to those feelings the enormous weight of guilt I carried over the things I had done in my quest to be accepted. I carried *that* heavy burden well into my adulthood.

For so long, I groveled in my mistakes, carrying around guilt, constantly begging God to forgive me. One day on my early morning prayer walk, I began to list my long inventory of failures before God and beg for His forgiveness.

After about thirty minutes of carrying around the heavy weight of guilt, I felt the Lord asking, "Are you done?"

I suddenly realized that I had spent the entire walk—a walk reserved for prayer and praise, a walk where God speaks to my heart, giving me direction and revelation—wallowing in guilt and shame. What a waste of time! Quickly, I asked the Lord to forgive me for constantly asking Him to forgive me. (You'll have to think about that one for a moment.)

Please don't get me wrong. I am not suggesting that we shouldn't confess our sins before God and repent of them. But we must realize that there is a big difference between conviction and condemnation.

Conviction comes from above. It is a sudden revelation that we have acted, spoken, or thought contrary to God's will. It pierces the heart and leads us to repent of our sins and head in a new direction. Conviction brings freedom and sets our feet on a path of victory.

Condemnation, on the other hand, comes from our insecurities about who we are in Christ Jesus—forgiven children of the King. Guilt, unlike conviction, is heavy. It weighs us down and hinders our steps. And you know what? It takes our focus off our Savior and puts it on ourselves. Kind of makes *us* idols, huh?

As I continued my morning walk, God showed me how He had already paid for my guilt, all of it. I didn't have to beg Him for forgiveness, and wallow before Him in shame. He'd taken that, too. Rather, God wanted me to come boldly before Him and just share my heart, so that He could share His with me. (Hebrews 4:16)

Remember, my friend, words of destruction, thoughts of defeat, and feelings of guilt are not God's idea of humility. They are Satan's tools to get us to hate ourselves so that we feel we are unworthy of God's love and unable to be used by Him. Satan wants us to be discouraged, frustrated, and disappointed with ourselves and with everyone around us. He knows it's impossible to love others to Christ when we are so focused on ourselves and our own shortcomings.

CHAPTER 18

KEEPING THE BIRDS
FROM NESTING

*We destroy every proud obstacle that keeps people
from knowing God. We capture their rebellious thoughts
and teach them to obey Christ.*
2 CORINTHIANS 10:5

It took me a long time to identify and unravel the wrong belief patterns
I accepted as truth during my childhood and teenage years. In fact, I am
still unraveling them as we speak. The battle for my mind is unending.
Satan attacks me daily, constantly tempting me to question my worth
and purpose by suggesting I haven't done enough or that I've failed something or someone in some way. Fortunately, I've now learned to recognize
these thoughts before they have the chance to take root and give place to
destruction.

Years ago, I heard an awesome saying that has been attributed to Martin
Luther: "You may not be able to keep birds from flying over your head, but
you can keep them from nesting in your hair."

Like birds soaring through the sky, defeating thoughts do, on occasion,
still zip through my mind. I'll probably never be completely free of them,
but I have learned how to prevent them from nesting in my heart and
mind. How? By choosing not to dwell on them, by refusing not to accept
them as truth, and by purposely filling my mind with godly thoughts so
there is no room for them to settle down. These three disciplines have

helped bring me into mental and emotional freedom. They've also been the key to staying free (John 8:32).

In order to avoid dwelling on half-truths and all-out-lies, I have had to train myself to recognize them. You've probably heard that people learn to identify counterfeit money by studying the real deal. By becoming intimately familiar with authentic money, they can identify fake currency, regardless of what form the counterfeit may take.

Likewise, in order to recognize a counterfeit thought (which, like counterfeit money, can appear in many forms), I've had to study the real deal. I've had to come to know God's thoughts intimately. This has required a discipline of truly studying God's Word rather than just merely skimming over it or being satisfied with little nuggets on Sunday morning. It's required getting alone with Him so that I can come into His presence and come to know His heart.

Saturating my mind with God's truth and applying it to my life has been the greatest investment I have ever made. Through His Word, I've learned about God's amazing love, His plan for my life, and the protection, provision, forgiveness, and power that is offered to me as His child. I've also learned who God is (and who He is not), and who I am in His eyes.

That, my friend, began to change everything. When I finally grasped the truth of who I was in Christ—the daughter of the Most High King, worth everything to Him, loved beyond measure, accepted and chosen not because of anything I have accomplished but simply because I am His child—the need to be somebody in the world's eye began to fade away.

Not only did I discover my identity and worth in Christ through His Word, I also became equipped with a supernatural weapon that has the power to both expose and pull down mental strongholds that block my ability to move forward into victory. (Read 2 Corinthians 10:4–5 and Ephesians 6.) God's weapon of truth enabled me, and continues to enable me, to quickly discern emotions and thoughts that are contrary to His purpose and will for my life.

Here is an example of how this plays out in my daily life. Fear is an emotion I meet often. Without a moment's notice, it can rise up in my heart and suddenly I fear failing in my endeavor, falling flat on my face, being hurt or rejected by people, or disappointing those I love.

In the past, this fear would sideline me for days, maybe even months. or cause me to change course. Now, however, I have learned to recognize this emotion and stomp out its fire before it has the opportunity to burst into full blaze and affect my destiny. This has come from learning to be conscious of my thoughts...to think about what I am thinking about, as evangelist Joyce Meyer often says.

When I notice my heart growing anxious, my mind churning, or that I am beginning to back down from something I had previously felt led to do, I stop and consider the why behind my what. A great illustration of this was during a recent trip to Russia.

Since adopting our children in 2005, I have felt the Lord leading me, on different occasions, to return to the orphanage where Dalton and Ivy once lived, in order to lavish His love on the women who work at the orphanage, as well as on the children who currently live there. Our visit to this remote region would prove to be a simple but powerful way to say thank you to these women for the gift of our children.

In 2013, I made my first trip back to the region of Glazov, and with the help of many ministry partners, blessed over a hundred women with Bibles in the Russian language, beautiful silk scarves, and handmade cards. The children were also given many exciting toys.

In addition to being reunited with the precious women who had raised our children and others who had been a part of our adoption process, I was also able to make a miraculous connection with the family who fosters Ivy's youngest sibling, Nikita.

Tim and I had attempted to adopt Nikita soon after we adopted Ivy. It was a lengthy process, but just as we were a month out from traveling to Russia to meet him, the government agency in charge of orphans placed

Nikita in a foster home with a local family. As a result, he was no longer available for adoption.

For years I had longed to meet this little boy. Now, by the grace of God, I was holding him in my lap, hearing in broken English the words, "Mama Kristi from America" as we zipped between snow-covered trees on a one-horse, open sleigh.

To top that off, with the help of my host, I located Ivy's older brother, Artur, in a remote camp for orphans, literally in the middle of a Russian forest. To say he was a bit shocked by my visit would be an understatement. I presented him with several small gifts and gave him a picture of our family with our contact information. Until our meeting, he had no idea of the whereabouts of his other siblings. It was an amazing trip.

As 2013 progressed, I felt God leading me back to Russia, but this time, I felt the desire to take Ivy with me. Her heart desperately longed to meet her brothers and to see the place where she had once lived. After much prayer, Tim and I felt this would be a wonderful opportunity for Ivy.

Once again, with the help of our ministry partners, we purchased scarves, toys, and other gifts to be presented to the women and orphans. We also made arrangements for a medical transport van to be purchased in Russia. Ivy and I would present this van, on behalf of our donors, during our trip.

For months, we prepared to go to Russia, raising funds and purchasing items. It was such a blessing to see my then eleven-year-old daughter stand before church congregations and school assemblies and share about her upcoming trip, and the opportunity she had to share God's love to children who lived where she once lived. To raise funds for the orphanage, Ivy made beautiful earrings that she sold at various events. And with the help of a friend, she made more than enough earrings to present to every woman at the orphanage as a special gift.

When all was said and done, Ivy had raised well over $1,000 in her efforts. I commended her on a job well done, to which she replied, "It's hard to resist cute." (Perhaps I should bring her on full-time to raise funds for the ministry!)

As the trip approached, however, doubts and questions began to rise up in my heart, bringing with them great fear. For many years, there has been much controversy over children adopted by Americans, so I worried. Would the Russian government try to take my daughter from me? Would we be safe alone on the seventeen-hour train ride from Moscow to the region where we were traveling? Would going back to the place she once lived as an orphan overwhelm Ivy with negative emotions? How would she handle meeting her two brothers?

Questions and scenarios began to play through my mind. Before I knew it, I was so anxious and overwhelmed that I had just about convinced myself to just ship the scarves and earrings overseas and let someone else present the van to the orphanage. The money had already been wired anyway; the van was already purchased. Did I really need to go?

Fortunately, I recognized what was happening before I cancelled my trip. I was being attacked by fear. As I took note of my anxious heart, I began to pray. I quickly realized that it wasn't God telling me not to go. No, my own fears and insecurities were telling me to stay home. The comments of well-meaning people, full of fear themselves, added fuel to the fire, causing me to question what I knew God had instructed me to do—minister hope and love to the Russian people.

Months later, on the other side of that trip, I could see why Satan attacked me so fiercely. He knew that the love of Christ would bring life, joy, and hope to many; and he was right. Many lives were impacted, including my daughter's, her brother's, and my own.

During this trip, Ivy was able to spend several action-packed days with Nikita, playing in the snow and eating Russian holiday delicacies. She even had a sleepover with him at his grandmother's home. That's my brave Ivy.

She also got to meet Artur, her older brother. God obviously had His hand in this meeting. Just listen to this: since my departure from Russia a year prior, I had not had any contact with Artur. But two days before Ivy and I were to return to America, Artur decided to send me an email, requesting an opportunity to meet his sister.

What's truly amazing is that Artur had no idea we were in Russia at the time. He was just looking at the family picture that I had given him the previous year and suddenly felt the courage to reach out to me. How surprised he was to find out that not only were we in Russia, but we already had plans to travel to the town where he resided! Incredibly, Ivy and Artur were reunited the very next day in a local pizza parlor.

Since our return home, Artur and I have regularly corresponded with the help of email and Google Translate. That alone is incredible, but wait, there's more! (Sounds like an infomercial, doesn't it?)

Through my new relationship with Artur, we have since learned the whereabouts of yet two more older siblings. Just recently, we received pictures of Ivy's brother and her sister, both of whom are in a local orphanage. Ivy and her sister, Angelina, are now sending selfies back and forth from one side of the globe to the other.

Talk about miracles! Five siblings, once scattered and isolated from each other, have now all been reunited. In the natural, this should have been impossible. How thankful I am that I got over my fear and obeyed the Lord so that Ivy and I could experience all these incredible blessings.

The only way this was possible was through the foundation of truth that had been established in my heart and mind. It's a foundation that I continually and consciously build and fortify through the daily study of God's Word. My knowledge of the Word enabled me to recognize that the emotion I was experiencing—fear—was not of God.

How did I know? Because Philippians 4:6–8 commands me to be anxious over nothing. Second Timothy 1:7 promises that God doesn't give me a spirit of fear, but a powerful, disciplined, and sound mind. Joshua

1:9 encourages me to be strong and courageous, while Philippians 4:13 reminds me that with God by my side, I can face and overcome anything. As I replaced my fearful thoughts with the above truths, I was able to move forward in peace and victory.

At first, this process of taking my thoughts captive was a full-time job. My mind had been a freight train of negative, condemning, fearful, guilt-ridden thoughts for so long that it naturally gravitated down a destructive path. I could go from praising the Lord to fearing for my life in a single moment. Sometimes I still can. Therefore, I must constantly monitor my thoughts. I must keep tabs on them and track not only where they are parked at the moment, but also where they have been and where they are getting ready to go.

As I've implemented this discipline and trusted the Lord, slowly but surely I have begun to enter God's rest...a place of mental and emotional peace that is totally undisturbed by my circumstances and those around me. What an amazing place to be.

SOMETHING TO THINK ABOUT

Before I move on, let me clarify something. Just as allowing fear to sideline you is not wise, foolishly pressing on isn't either. We are, as the Bible says, to be as wise as a serpent and as gentle as a dove while moving forward in this world (Matthew 10:16). We are to follow the Lord's leading at all times.

There have been many times when I've had to rearrange my plans and change my course. For example, in 2015, a year after the incredible trip described above, I cancelled my trip to Russia, even though I already had my plane ticket in hand. I just didn't have a peace about going.

Unlike 2014, where the desire to cancel my trip was due to my fearful, anxious heart, this time around it was a result of the absence of God's peace. There is a huge difference.

Peace is from God, a fruit of the Holy Spirit, who resides within us. He quickens our hearts to aid us in our decision-making processes (Colossians 3:15). A lack of peace is a great indicator that perhaps we should put on the brakes and seek some answers.

Fear, however, is from Satan. It creates scenarios in our minds, anxieties in our hearts, physical and mental sickness, as well as confusion and chaos in our lives. People ruled by fear either shrink back or perhaps rush carelessly ahead. In the end, fear leads nowhere, except away from God's best for our lives. Satan knows it is impossible to walk with God while drowning in a sea of fear. Fear and faith are, after all, complete opposites. And without faith, it is impossible to please God (Hebrews 11:6).

One must discern between the two when making a decision. In regard to my trip, I perceived no hint of anxiety in my heart or wild scenarios playing through my mind, swaying me to stay put. Therefore, I knew that fear was not the culprit.

In fact, I actually wanted to go, and so did Ivy. Our Russian host and Ivy's siblings were excitedly awaiting our arrival, too. But even in all of this,

I just couldn't move forward. I sensed that I should stay home and celebrate the new year with my husband and sons—something I had missed the previous two years.

Additionally, I realized that in the excitement of my planning, I hadn't even asked God if I should go. Instead, I had booked my ticket assuming He would want me to return to Russia during the holiday season and share His love as I had in the past. (Russians celebrate Christmas on January 7th.) There was so much to be gained in going.

You know, there *was* much to be gained in going, but there was also much to be gained in staying. You should have seen the kids and me bringing in the new year together. I don't know how Tim slept through all the commotion. I will treasure that time forever.

Friend, in your faith journey, there are two things you must constantly do: push through fear and pursue peace. As you pray for discernment and take the time to listen to the Spirit of God, He will always reveal the direction you should go.

CHAPTER 19

JESUS, TAKE THE WHEEL!

Don't copy the behavior and customs of this world, but let
God transform you into a new person by changing the way
you think. Then you will learn to know God's will for you,
which is good and pleasing and perfect.

ROMANS 12:2

I now had the discipline of taking my thoughts captive in operation, but I still faced the task of surrendering my actions to the Lord. I needed to give God complete control of my life—to truly get behind Him and let Him lead.

This wouldn't come easily.

The process of complete surrender actually began in January of 2013, during my first trip back to Russia. At that time, circumstances arose in the ministry that brought me to a crossroads. I had a choice to make—either I could continue to persevere stubbornly through the chaos of sickness, pain, confusion, and exhaustion; or I could stop the insanity and give God the controls of my life, once and for all.

For years I had known there were changes I needed to make in my priorities and commitments, and even in the organization of the ministry. Yet I had avoided them, ignoring the Lord and dismissing the wisdom of my husband and other trusted people.

As a performer and people pleaser, these changes would be difficult and uncomfortable to implement. They would require discipline, living purposely, and letting go. Not to mention, they had the potential to offend, let down, and possibly even hurt people I loved.

After much prayer, however, and consideration of my current state and past experiences, I finally relinquished the controls and surrendered my will to God's. Not just in theory, but in practice.

With the following prayer, I got behind the boat—God—and determined to follow His lead, even if it meant going back to the starting dock and rebuilding my life and the ministries from the ground up. Which is exactly what I had to do.

"Lord," I prayed, "I surrender everything I have to You. Take it all—the ministries, my family, my life, my relationships—they're Yours. Take the controls; I don't want them anymore. I've driven long enough and often made a mess of things. I refuse to take another step forward unless I know You're leading the way."

No longer did I want to rely on my know-how, creativity, strength, or resources. Never again did I want to live trying to please people and perform for those around me. I was done with it all. I was ready to let Jesus take the wheel.

After my prayer of surrender, I invited Tim to what I would call a "come to Jesus meeting." You know, one of those meetings where you get real with one another, face the truth of what is going on, and determine a course of action for change. With tears in my eyes, I asked Tim, in total sincerity, to give me wisdom of how to move forward.

"Tell me what I should do," I asked.

For years I had overlooked Tim's advice, usually running to friends or other people within the organization—people I knew would give me their approval to move forward with what I thought was a good idea. I was so certain that I had my orders from God that I didn't want anyone, not even my husband, interfering with the direction I felt led to go.

In this place of surrender, my eyes were finally opened to the wise counsel God had given me in my husband. Praise God, my heart was willing to receive it. The Lord revealed how I could trust Tim's love for me and our family, and also his ability to hear from God to lead us. I cannot explain the relief that came over me as I rested in this newfound trust.

I asked Tim to forgive me for putting other people's advice and my own desires above his. I also asked God to forgive me. Then, I asked Tim to lead our family as God intended. He accepted my apology and invitation to lead.

Over the weeks and months that followed, Tim and I, in total unity, sought the Lord's direction for our lives and for the ministries He had given to us both. We met with our Board of Directors in regard to the direction of the ministry, as well as with mentors who helped direct us as a couple and as parents. During this time, Tim began to open up and share his thoughts and opinions about many things. I listened, agreeing to take the steps Tim suggested.

First on the agenda? Officially turning over the leadership of In His Wakes to the current director, Nate Miller. Tim felt it was time for me to step down and let Nate—the one God was now calling to lead IHW on a daily basis—lead, so that every vision God had purposed for me could come to fruition. Tim then encouraged me to focus on developing my God-given gifts of writing, singing, and speaking—something that I couldn't do if I continued to lead IHW. Tim could sense that God had incredible plans for IHW and the other ministries God had placed on my heart, if I would just let go and get focused. Hearing Tim's heart, feeling his support, and perceiving his confidence that I had gifts that could touch many lives gave me the courage to release my baby, IHW.

Next, Tim and I discussed the various activities of KOJ Ministries. Together, we decided that in addition to letting IHW go, it was also time to release the local resource center, Champion's Heart. There was no denying that the responsibility of having a staff as well as a large facility and grounds to maintain was affecting our family and my health. It was also draining our resources and causing strife, not only in our home but in other relationships that were dear to me. Running a center wasn't my calling, nor was it my passion. Speaking, singing, and writing, on the other hand, were. And while in the midst of operating in those gifts, I experienced nothing but joy.

Releasing the center wasn't as easy as I imagined. My fear of people's opinions began to surface. What would people in our community think if I stepped away from the vision that I had so passionately shared? Wasn't that failure?

After some time, I realized the answer to that question was no. Moving forward obediently with God in a new direction was not a failure. In fact, it was guaranteeing success (Joshua 1:7).

I moved forward with a clean conscience, knowing that I had given wholeheartedly of my time, resources, and energy to Champion's Heart. I had no regrets. I had met so many wonderful people during my journey with this resource center. It was also in that place that I found the courage and support to begin *Victorious Living*, a magazine that would soon touch tens of thousands of lives. God has used every experience to mold and make me into the person I am today.

Did I do everything perfectly as a leader? No. Should I have done some things differently? With hindsight, most definitely. But at the time and in the midst of it all, I can say that I did the best I could. I loved the people around me, and I loved the Lord. Those two things were my motivation.

As for the mistakes? Well...like in skiing, I learn from them. Already they are helping me be a better leader and wiser servant in my current endeavors.

The last change Tim and I felt the Lord leading us to make was to move our family and the administration of IHW and KOJM to Central Florida. Although we had tossed around the idea of moving from Keystone Heights in the past, we hadn't truly felt it was possible due to our commitments to Champion's Heart. Now that God had released us from the center, it was time. We placed a for sale sign in our yard, as well as on every piece of property we owned in the area, and began our search for a new home for our family and a new school for our children.

There were times I grieved over the loss of what had once been, but my heart grew increasingly confident about the future. I had such peace and joy, even in the midst of some difficult transitions. Our entire family was excited about the new thing that God had on the horizon. Even our dogs, Mater and Bear, were wagging their tails as they sensed us preparing for this new adventure. While none of us knew what lay ahead, we trusted that whatever it was, it would be good.

SOMETHING TO THINK ABOUT

Because of fear and my desire to please those around me, I have often rebelled against what I knew God desired me to do. Instead, I have held on to what and who was comfortable at the time. Not only did I rebel against God, I also ignored the advice of wise, godly people, especially that of my faithful husband, Tim.

Looking back, I can see with certainty the great cost that my disobedience brought to my health and to my relationships. It led our family and ministry into chaos and depleted every ounce of my energy and joy.

When I finally humbled myself before the Lord, and my husband, and did what I knew I was supposed to do, God lifted me up and enabled me to break through cycles of sickness, confusion, exhaustion, and frustration that had lasted for over a decade. My marriage and my relationship with my children blossomed. Every ministry division flourished beyond imagination, and my health was restored. Within months of taking those hard steps of obedience, my stomach pain began to subside, my energy levels increased, and my mind became focused and alert.

Here is my point, and please don't miss it. You can say "Hit it, God!" till you are blue in the face, but if you don't listen to Him and do what He is telling you to do, you will not rise up out of the water for very long. I am a living testimony that all the doctors, disciplined exercise, food routines, structured schedules, and even all the prayer and scripture in the world will not bring healing unless complete obedience to God is there as well.

Is there something the Lord is requiring of you? Perhaps He is leading you to release a tangible item like a facility or ministry. Or, perhaps an emotion like anger, bitterness, unforgiveness, fear, or guilt. He may even be urging you to let go of someone. Remember, you cannot ignore the instructions of the Lord and expect to walk in the fullness of His blessings.

CHAPTER 20

SENT TO PRISON

I was in prison, and you visited me.
MATTHEW 25:36

With preparations for our move being made and the responsibilities of leading In His Wakes systematically being handed over to Nate, I felt such excitement. For years I had been living under the heavy, burdensome, constant pressure of making these ministries successful. Now in this place of surrender, I found freedom as I trusted that the Lord would supernaturally place me exactly where He desired me to be.

This transition was tough, I must admit, but I didn't mind all the tedious work because I knew I was being faithful in the place where God wanted me to be at *that* moment. No longer was it about pressing forward to arrive at some preconceived destination. No longer was it about preparing for some ministry event or doing something. It was simply about being where God wanted me to be at that moment (and enjoying it), and loving on those He had placed before me—most importantly, my family.

With the pressure of *doing* subsiding, I was finally free to embrace the incredible ministry God had given me as a wife and mother. Now please don't get me wrong—during all the ministry's formative years, I was a good wife and mother. I loved Tim and our kids so much and took care of their needs. They were, by no means, neglected.

Inside of me, however, there had been a constant struggle. If I was with my kids, I felt like I needed to be at an event or at the office ministering to someone else. Likewise, when I was ministering, I felt guilty for not being home with my kids. I couldn't win.

In this place of surrender, I suddenly felt free. And relaxed. Even those around me could detect the change. No longer was I running around doing, just for the sake of doing. Suddenly, there was no rush to get anywhere. God knew where we were going and when we should arrive; therefore, I reasoned I could trust Him to bring it all to fruition.

In this new place of rest, I promised the Lord I would no longer charge forward. Instead, I would focus on staying close to Him, listen for His voice, and step only through the doors He opened. While I waited patiently, God began to open doors for me to minister to an audience I would never have considered—prisoners.

Not long after, He sent me to prison, too!

Here's how it happened. In the spring of 2013, a lady from Missouri received a copy of our ministry's magazine, *Victorious Living*. After reading it, she forwarded it to her friend, Bill Doyle, who was serving a seventeen-year sentence in a federal prison in Miami.

Bill, previously a professional wake board driver, had been very involved in the water-sports industry prior to his arrest. This lady thought he would enjoy our publication as it was published by a water-skier. I'm not sure whether she knew at the time, but Bill and I were personally acquainted, as we had ministered together in 2004 at several IHW events. His testimony had even been included in our *Making the Cut* devotional.

Upon receiving the magazine, Bill wrote me a letter. In it, he humbly asked for forgiveness for any harm his actions had caused our ministry. I accepted Bill's apology and immediately wrote him back. Over the next several months, we corresponded often.

In August of 2013, while in South Florida for a water-ski event, I decided to visit Bill. Until that time, I hadn't even considered entering the doors of a prison. Yet, there I was.

As I walked into the waiting room of the security area, my heart raced with excitement. I could sense God was about to rock my world.

Anyone in the room could see I was obviously new to this experience. I filled out the required paperwork, then I sat down and waited to be called. Next to me was a sweet lady who was waiting to visit her son. As we talked, I learned that she made the long trip from Orlando to visit him every weekend. She was very excited about the fact that he would be getting out soon. How shocked I was to find out her excitement was about an event that would take place over a year and a half away!

Eventually, it was my turn to walk through security and then be led in a single-file line to the visiting area, where I would meet with my friend whom I hadn't seen in over eight years. I watched the reunion of loved ones all around me, and I found myself overwhelmed by the realization that *this is reality* for so many people—a reality so foreign to me.

As I waited for my friend, I asked the Lord to reveal to me what He saw in this place of darkness. He answered my prayer, showing me so much that I could barely contain myself.

In that moment, God gave me supernatural eyes to see past the inmates' brown jumpsuits, identification numbers, and crimes, and to see what He saw—people. People loved by Him; so much so that He sent His Son, Jesus, to give His life for their pardon, just as He had done for me (John 3:16).

To God, these were people, no more a criminal than I am. "For everyone has sinned; we all fall short of God's glorious standard" (Romans 3:23). They were fathers, sons, husbands, brothers, and friends, treasured by my Lord. Just like me, they had been handcrafted in God's image for good works. Their God-given destinies, however, had been sidelined by circumstances and bad choices. I sensed God wanting to resurrect those buried gifts and passions for His glory.

With God's eyes, I saw before me hundreds of people in desperate need of the Father's hope, encouragement, grace, healing, reconciliation, and love. People who needed the message of "hit it" more than anyone.

While I was still processing these truths, I met with Bill. And as we conversed, God revealed yet another truth—the power of a visit. My taking the time to see Bill was life-changing for him. I could hear it in his voice; I could see it in his tears. Bill later told me that those few moments I spent with him had given him the encouragement he needed to carry on another day. They had also boosted his faith and renewed his hope in Christ.

As I drove away, headed back to my reality, I wept. I wept over the families that had been torn apart. I wept over the weight of my friend's guilt and shame and his struggle of accepting God's forgiveness. I wept over his fear of not making it out of prison alive. I wept over the stories he shared with me about the men that sat within a stone's throw from us. God had opened my eyes—it was yet another *aha* moment.

"I see, God." I whispered. "Now what?"

Knowing my passionate heart's tendency to get ahead of God, I added these words. "Lord, I am willing to go wherever You want me to go...even to prison. But I am not pushing my way through those doors. If You want me in prison, then I need You to send me there."

Well...He did. And very quickly, I might add.

Within a week of my prison experience, I was invited to lunch by one of my board members who wanted me to meet his friend, Mr. Thomas Johnson. Turns out, Thomas, a former New York pimp and drug dealer, was very involved with prison ministry, and had been for seventeen years.

Through this new relationship, prison gates began to swing wide open. Within a couple of weeks, I had a registration number that gave me the ability to enter any Florida State Prison as a minister. The director of the chaplaincy office at the Department of Corrections placed a request that *Victorious Living* be distributed in every prison in Florida.

Soon, opportunities to speak to inmates young and old, men and women, began to present themselves. In fact, the day I received my registration number, I received an invitation to speak to male youth offenders, ages fourteen to twenty-four, who would soon be released.

As I prepared for my visit, I sat before the Lord and asked Him to pour into my heart the message He would have me deliver to these young men—men the world would say aren't worth a dime. God answered my prayer. Suddenly, He prompted my heart with words that began to bubble up in my spirit. As I wrote the following, my fingers could hardly keep up!

My child, I gave up My life for you. If you had been the only person on this earth, I still would have come and laid down My life for you. Why? Because you are precious to Me. You are the object of My love. You are worth everything to Me, even My life.

When I look at you, I am filled with joy. I see not the failures of your past. Rather, I see the plans I have for your future. And they are good!

You've been told you'll never amount to anything, that you'll never make it. You've been told you're a mistake, a failure, and a disappointment. You've been told you're alone and without hope. But I say different!

I say you are fearfully and wonderfully made. I created you with My own hands. I breathed life into your unformed body. And I don't make mistakes.

When I created the whole world, I saw you. I saw every day of your life before one of them came to be, and I still desired to create you. I smiled at the very thought of you, for I saw what you could become in Me. I saw the gifts and talents I had placed within you that have the potential to change the world for My kingdom!

It matters not what you've done, where you've come from, or where you've been. It matters not what possessions you hold in your hand. It matters not what people have said. If I am for you, nothing can stop you. And I am for you. In Me, you are victorious! No power of hell, no scheme of man, no past mistake can stop the plans I have for you.

So rise up, My child; I am with you. In Me, you have all you need. I know your fears, doubts, and your pain. Give them all to Me, and rest. Be anxious over nothing, for you are not alone. I walk before you and lead the way...follow Me. I walk beside you and uphold you with My righteous right hand, keeping you stable and moving you forward. Hold on; never let go of Me. I will never let go of you. I'll never leave you or forsake you.

I walk behind you. I've got your back, so you don't have to look back! Fear not. Move forward, I am protecting you, fighting your battles. You don't have to seek revenge. I've got your back, and I'll make right what is wrong.

Forget the past and focus on your future—it is good! It will not always be easy, but in Me, you will be victorious. I will give you the strength to take every step and overcome every trial. I'll give you the wisdom to make every decision. I'll provide for your every need. I'll also give you the desires of your heart and help you fulfill the call on your life. I will never fail you.

Listen not to the voices of the world or the voices in your head. Focus not on the difficult circumstances and battles ahead. Listen only to Me, to My truth. The truth is, I love you with an everlasting love. The truth is, you are forgiven. The truth is, I have great plans for you. The truth is, nothing is impossible!

Grab hold of My truth. Grab hold of My hand and move forward with Me. I will not disappoint you.

With the above letter in hand, I walked through the facility's security gate. When I heard the metal door slam behind me, the same excitement that I had experienced seeing Bill rose again in my heart. Amazingly, there was no fear; only peace and joy and anticipation over what God was getting ready to do. I knew it was going to be powerful. And it was.

I stood there before hundreds of inmates, encouraging their hearts with the Word of God, His love letter, and with the song, "Redeemed," by Big Daddy Weave. And those men sat on the edge of their seats, many with tears streaming down their faces, taking every word to heart. There was no denying it: this was definitely good soil. I've spoken at hundreds of venues in my lifetime, yet never before had I been in the presence of people so hungry for hope and truth, so desperate for God's unconditional love. It was an incredible, life-changing event for all of us.

Within the months that followed, *Victorious Living* made its way into nearly every Florida prison. It also landed in the hands of people who have great influence in the prison system and who lead large international prison ministries. One by one, they have come to me, extending their hand of partnership, inviting me to be a part what God is doing. Before I knew it, I was standing in front of thousands of inmates as a platform speaker for these established ministries, sharing the message of "hit it!"

With the magazine circulating through the prison system, letters soon arrived attesting to the power of the testimonies published in *Victorious Living*. These stories were encouraging many in their faith. Inmate after inmate shared how they had come to know the Lord through *Victorious Living*. Others requested discipleship so that they could grow spiritually.

With the amount of letters increasing daily (more than I could possibly read much less respond to), I sensed the need for a prison correspondence team. With prayer, the Lord led me straight to a precious lady with a heart to extend God's love and grace to those behind the wire. With the help of Linda and a team of faithful believers, hundreds of inmates are being encouraged and equipped to live a life of victory.

Since my first visit with Bill, God has continued to open doors, making it ever so clear that prison ministry is part of His will for my life. He alone has placed me, as well as the magazine, in the prison system. And I'm so thankful.

In this short journey already, I've met so many incredible people who have decades of knowledge in the area of prison ministry and many of whom have experienced life behind prison walls. I sense the Lord saying, "Learn from them."

My new friends are living witnesses of the redemptive and transformative power of Christ. People often ask me if I really think people can change. Yes, I know they can! In Christ and through Christ, people can live victorious lives, no matter their past.

In regard to all of the above, this former pro water-skier, now mother of three, and forever a southern girl, can only say one thing, "Who woulda ever thunk it?" Certainly not Bill or me. We are both excited to know that a legacy is being created far beyond the ones we have left in our sports.

SOMETHING TO THINK ABOUT

I've been ministering full-time now for over a decade. As I've already shared, I've learned how important it is to move forward with God in His timing and in His strength. There is nothing more important than being where He is so that we can go where He goes.

Many times in the past, spurred on by my excitement and passion for God, I have run ahead of Him in my pursuit to fulfill the call He has placed on my life. In the end, I've usually found myself exhausted and unfortunately, I've sometimes made a mess of things. The Lord, however, in His mercy and grace, has graciously covered my mistakes and patiently taught me a better way.

With KOJM's new prison outreach, I'm committed to move forward with God in this better way. I don't want to take one step apart from Him. I don't want to move ahead, nor do I want to lag behind. As Galatians 5:25 says, I want to live by the Spirit and keep in step with Him.

Side by side. Walking in step with the Holy Spirit. That's where I want to be.

To do this, God has shown me that I have to be fully present with Him and fully in His presence at all times. As I have made these two things my priority, I've seen God do what only God can do.

You know, my old way of thinking would tell me that taking time away from doing would cause me to lag behind in fulfilling the dreams God has placed on my heart. But the powerful truth is that as I've taken time to seek God's face and to worship in His presence, God has been working behind the scenes of my life. He has brought about resources and relationships, orchestrated connections, and provided opportunities galore. Whatever and whoever I have needed, He has provided.

Are there steps you've been trying to take on your own? Doors you've been trying to force open? Take a step back, my friend, and get in the presence of God. Trust Him to make a way, and when He does, walk through those doors with Him. Blessings await!

CHAPTER 21

A HEART LIKE DREW'S

*The eyes of the Lord search the whole earth in order to
strengthen those whose hearts are fully committed to him.*
2 CHRONICLES 16:9

Over the last few chapters, I've shared with you many lessons and revelations that have helped me continue to move forward in life. As you've no doubt noticed, I have made many mistakes.

Every day, in some fashion, I have failed as a mother, wife, daughter, friend, or ministry leader. I've made poor judgment calls in just about every area of my life. I can't even begin to count the number of times I've gotten ahead of God in my decision making.

Yet, as I've made the decision to focus on God instead of my failures and to accept His forgiveness instead of wallow in condemnation and guilt, I can humbly say that God has used my life in unique and incredible ways, despite and even in the midst of my mess-ups. I can only smile in amazement as I realize that, just like the falls I experienced as a water-skier didn't prevent me from becoming a world champion, the falls I have experienced as a child of God haven't prevented me from becoming His champion either.

How? Because of a willing heart. More than anything, I want to follow after God and be used by Him. I may not always follow Him perfectly, but God knows I'm willing, and with everything I have within me, I'm trying.

Please don't misinterpret the above and think that I'm trying to earn God's favor, love, or approval; or that I'm trying to work my way to Heaven.

Scripture is very clear that God's love and eternal salvation are not based on performance. Rather, they are based on His grace as exhibited through the sacrifice of His Son. Ephesians 2:8–10 says,

> God saved you by His grace when you believed. And you can't take credit for this; it is a gift from God. Salvation is not a reward for the good things we have done, so none of us can boast about it. For we are God's masterpiece. He has created us anew in Christ Jesus, so we can do the good things He planned for us long ago.

But there is an element of daily trying. Faith without works is dead. See James 2. Every day I must choose to humble myself to obey God's Word and the promptings of His Holy Spirit, even when they lead me out of my comfort zones.

Every day I must decide to serve those around me. Every day I must choose to praise God, even when my heart is breaking. Every day I must draw close to Him through the study of His Word, become involved with a community of other believers, listen with an open heart, and pray. See my point?

Coming into an intimate relationship with Jesus Christ doesn't just happen. Yes, salvation occurs the moment we put our faith and trust in Him, but from that point forward, there is an element of effort involved if we want to truly know Him, to be used by Him, and to receive His best for our lives. We can't simply rely on our conversion experience from days, weeks, months, years, or even decades ago to sustain us in our Christian journey. Trust me, I've tried.

As I began to make an effort to grow in my faith, an amazing thing happened. I grew! And I've continued to grow and be transformed as I've continued to try…as I've been willing to say, "hit it, God!" over and over again.

Do you recall that Krispy Kreme doughnut illustration I used in the introduction to this book? In it I gave a humorous description of the doughnut's transformation from a clump of dough to a hot, sugar-drizzled delicacy.

Similarly, the Christian life is a process of transformation. We start out, like those delicious doughnuts, as a clump of dough. Yet as we place ourselves in the Master's hands, we begin to be transformed into something beautiful, tasty even, to the world.

Like the clump of dough as it bumps along the conveyor belt heading to that glaze of glory, however, we can sometimes fall. But that's okay. Unlike the baker, God doesn't consider us contaminated, and He doesn't throw us in the trash bin! No, in His grace, He welcomes us back with arms wide open, ready once again to make and mold us. All He needs from us is a willingness to get back on the conveyor belt of transformation with Him.

My friend, that's all God is looking for. He's not looking for perfection. He's simply looking for a heart that is willing to try again. One who will listen, learn, repent, and persevere through the falls. He's looking for a heart that is willing to say "Hit it, God!" Through that heart, God can touch the world!

Years ago at an In His Wakes event, God showed me a beautiful example of the kind of heart He desires. I had just returned the boat to shore to pick up the next knee boarder when a young boy named Drew called out, "Miss Kristi, can I ride in the boat and help?"

I could see his eagerness and desire, so I invited him to come along for the ride. I gave Drew some instruction and safety tips that he obeyed to the best of his ability with both excitement and enthusiasm. I smiled as I watched him run to the back of the boat and pull the rope in with every bit of strength and energy he had in his small frame.

After a few minutes I said, "Drew, thank you so much for being willing to ride in the boat and help me."

"Of course!" he replied. "I love boats, and I love the water. This is where I want to be!"

After we'd pulled the last child on the kneeboard, I asked Drew if he wanted to ride. I could sense he was about to explode with eagerness to get back on the water, but he contained himself and said, "I've already had a turn."

"That's okay," I said. "It will be your reward for helping me."

His face beamed with the biggest smile I had ever seen as he hopped out of the boat, got situated on the board, and yelled for me to go. I took off and watched with joy as this young boy climbed up on his knees and began to cut back and forth on the board.

After a few minutes, I stopped the boat and said, "Drew, why don't you try a trick on the board, perhaps a 180 or a 360?"

"What do you mean?" he asked.

I shut down the engine and showed him how to maneuver the board in various directions.

"Okay, I'll try!" he said excitedly.

After getting up on the board, Drew got a serious look on his face and attempted what I had shown him. He fell on his first attempt.

As I turned the boat back around, I was expecting to pick up a disappointed child. But to my surprise, Drew just laughed aloud and exclaimed, "I tried, Miss Kristi! I didn't make it, but I tried!"

"You did great, Drew!" I encouraged him. Then I gave him instructions on how to correct his mistake.

Drew tried the trick a few more times, getting closer and closer each time. After a few minutes, however, I got a radio call from our program director, Nate Miller.

"Kristi, are you coming back anytime soon?" Nate asked jokingly.

I had known that call would eventually come, but I was having so much fun with Drew, I just figured I'd stay out there until I got called back to shore. It is so rare to find a person eager to help others, eager to give of their energy and time, willing to listen to instruction, willing to try new things, and willing to persevere through the falls. I was having the time of my life. I could have stayed out there with Drew all day.

Just being in his presence brought joy to my heart and made me want to share my heart of wisdom about water sports with him. I also wanted to give him the desire of his heart—in this case, another whirl around on the kneeboard—as that in itself brought me joy.

As I spent time on the water with this amazing child, God spoke to my heart, "This is how I feel about you."

For many years, I had envisioned God as a harsh judge, constantly disappointed in me, eager to bring down His gavel of judgment when I failed. I also felt I had to beg Him to give me good things in my life.

But there I sat in the boat, looking at that wet child fumbling clumsily around on the kneeboard, and I suddenly realized that, just as I was enjoying being with Drew, God enjoys spending time with me. And just as I enjoyed blessing Drew and teaching him new things, God enjoys blessing me and sharing His heart with me so that I can go higher and higher in Him.

For the first time, I understood that God is thrilled beyond measure when I run to Him and ask, "Can I come on the journey with You and be a part of what You are doing? Will You teach me everything You know? Can I try again?"

As I fumble around on my spiritual kneeboard, often without a clue as to what I am doing, God is in the boat, grinning from ear to ear, pointing me out to His angels, and saying, "Look at her go! That's *My girl!*"

And that's my God—a loving, kind, generous, forgiving God of second chances. And you know what? He can be your God, too.

My friend, God's not mad at us when we fall or don't understand what we are doing as we go through this thing called life. In fact, it's just the opposite. As long as we are putting our faith in Him and giving it a go, He is pleased. He is blessed beyond measure when He meets a child open to listen, eager to learn, and willing to try. And when He finds someone like that, His greatest desire is to bless our socks off by giving us His time, His wisdom, and His blessings.

SOMETHING TO THINK ABOUT

The life of David gives a perfect example of an imperfect person being used by God. You've most likely heard about God's reference to David as a man after His own heart (Acts 13:22). But did you know that David was an adulterer, a murderer, and a parent with major childrearing issues? Check him out in Second Samuel. It's an amazing study.

So what could God have possibly meant when He referred to David in this way? Allow me to give you my idea of what God was saying here. I imagine Him saying,

"I have chosen David because he is a man who will never let his circumstances, injustices, fears, or failures stop him from chasing after My heart and doing My will. He is a man who in the midst of his confusion will nonetheless say to Me, 'Hit it, God! I trust You.'

"He's a man who will boldly stand before the giant Goliath when the odds are piled high against him and proclaim, 'Hit it, God! You will give me the victory.'

"When he fails, he will come to repentance, receive My forgiveness, and humbly say, 'Hit it, God! I'm sorry. Can we go again?'

"When he can't seem to hear My voice, he will quiet his mind at My feet and ask, 'Lord, will You please search my heart and show me any areas of my life where I am off course so we can take off again?'

"When he is attacked and falsely accused by those around him, David will rise up courageously and say, 'Hit it, God! You are my Protector.' When he is in need, he will look to the heavens in trust and say, 'Hit it, God! You are my Provider.'

"David is a man who will continually praise and give thanks to My name. He is a man after My own heart! This is the man I choose because this is the type of man I can use."

David was *chosen* to be used by God because he had a heart that *chased consistently after* the heart of God. He was a man who kept pressing forward through his mistakes, confusion, obstacles, rejection, isolation, and pain, faithfully seeking God and His will.

Oh, I want to be like David! I want to be a person who seeks after the heart of God every day of my life. I want to be the one who refuses to let circumstances, people, emotions, and mistakes keep me from keeping on. I know without a doubt that as long as I continually say "Hit it, God," there is no power of hell or scheme of man that can stop His purposes and plans from coming to fruition in my life. And the same holds true for you.

—◁∅∅▷—

CHAPTER 22

PRESS ON!

No, dear brothers and sisters, I have not achieved it,
but I focus on this one thing:
Forgetting the past and looking forward to what lies ahead,
I press on to reach the end of the race and receive the heavenly prize
for which God, through Christ Jesus, is calling us.
PHILIPPIANS 3:13–14

My granddaddy Charlie used to tell me, "It takes a long time to become a champion, baby." Boy, was he ever right!

It took twenty-five years from the first time I skimmed across the waters until I stood on the podium where I was crowned World Champion. Victory is a journey, and sometimes it's easy, but sometimes it can grow steep, tiring, and overwhelming.

There were years when I thought I'd fail to achieve my goals, but because I refused to quit and because I refused to allow my emotions to dictate my choices, victory came. Life takes the same determination.

Be assured, this thing called a Christian walk isn't going to be easy. Satan will make sure of it. But as you completely remove the option of quitting from your life, and as you commit to say "Hit it!" to God over and over again, victory will come. It may not come immediately, but it will come. Take it from me: your victory is always around the bend. In fact, it may just be only one "hit it!" away.

Throughout this book I've shared many of my failures and the lessons I've learned from them. As we near the end of our journey together, I'd like to finish on a positive note by sharing the disciplines that helped lead me to success in the midst of those mistakes. Many of these have been discussed already, but I want to group them all together for quick reference.

Whether as an athlete or in a relationship with the Lord, the keys to victory are the same. Below are several things that led me to the top of the podium as a water-skier. Ironically, they are the same actions that will lead us all to the top of God's podium—that place of victory where we experience God's best, and the place where He is glorified, lives are impacted, and where we consistently experience His joy and peace.

Here are those keys to victory.

PURPOSE TO BE A CHAMPION

As a little girl, I purposed in my heart to become a champion water-skier, regardless of the sacrifices required. For the next thirty years, I made life decisions aimed at moving toward that one goal, and I guarded myself from anything that could become a distraction. This commitment paid off.

Similarly, victory in my Christian walk began the day I purposed in my heart to get off my spiritual dock, follow after God wholeheartedly, and make daily life decisions that would move me closer to Him.

The undeniable truth is that there is no such thing as a half-committed champion in any arena of life, regardless whether it's in athletics, business, marriage, finances, parenting, education, physical health, or a Christian walk. Victory begins with a decision and is achieved through a daily commitment to line up your life decisions with actions that have the ability to move you toward your goal.

GET OFF THE DOCK DAILY

As an athlete, I made a daily decision to get off the ski dock and move out onto the water, regardless of how I felt emotionally or physically. Nothing could keep me off the water, not even the stern warnings of medical doctors. You could say that I was crazy when it came to my commitment to be a champion.

Does this mean I woke up every morning and said, "Yippee, I get to train today?"

No way! Most days I woke up to a body racked by physical pain. Sometimes the weather was atrocious. Who likes to ski in the wind, cold, or rain? Many times I simply wanted to go play with my friends and be a normal teenager.

Nonetheless, despite my physical conditions and wavering emotions, there were very few days where I stayed on the dock. Even at tournaments, as I waited for my turn on the water with knees quaking, mouth drying, fear mounting, and stomach stabbing, I would still choose to jump into the water and give it my all. Why? Because I knew that victory would only come as a result of my decision to get off the dock. And I wanted victory.

Similarly, in my Christian walk, victory has only come with my willingness to push through my emotions, fleshly desires, and yes, even physical and emotional pain and to move out onto the waters with Christ daily. Just like in skiing, I don't always feel like it.

Most certainly, there are days when I'd prefer to stay in bed, watch TV instead of study my Bible, and eat instead of fast or take a prayer walk. There are days when I guess you could say I'd just like to be a normal person.

I've learned, however, that I can't allow my feelings to dictate my choices. Just like in skiing, if I want victory, if I want to experience God's best and live a life of impact, I have to be committed to this goal daily. Victory doesn't just happen.

GET UP WHEN YOU FALL

Even with commitment, I still experienced falls. Every day as I moved toward my goal of being a champion water-skier, whether I was a state, regional, national, or world champion, I fell.

Sometimes I found myself in the water because of my own mistakes; sometimes it was the result of external conditions; and at other times it was the result of other people's actions. But regardless of the reason behind the fall, I still made the choice to get up and say, "Hit it!" again and again and again.

Similarly, as a believer, victory will only come when we choose to persevere, refusing to let our falls hinder our commitment to move forward. Life is tough. It can send waves that overwhelm us and knock us right off our feet. People send waves, too. Even our own choices can trip us up.

Regardless of the cause, however, we must determine to keep getting up. We must be willing to consistently say "Hit it!"—no matter how hard or how painful the falls.

Learn from Your Mistakes

To state the obvious, falls hurt. As a water-skier, tumbling across the water on my head at speeds in excess of 60 mph impacted every part of my physical body. To this day, I still feel the consequences of those falls in just about every joint. But you know what? When I refused to let those falls keep me face down in the water and when I chose instead to learn from them, victory eventually came.

Falls, no matter how big or how painful, do not have to dictate our destinies. If we are teachable, they can be the very lessons we need to move one step closer to the goal. As an athlete, I viewed my mistakes as opportunities to learn. From those lessons, I could avoid future mishaps by moving forward differently. With my new knowledge, I was also able to help others overcome the same mistakes.

Similarly, as believers, if we learn from instead of wallow in our mistakes, we can continue to move forward. I am not discounting our responsibility to avoid sin and to live a holy life, but we are human. We are imperfect beings who will, at some point in our lives, screw up in the way we think, react, speak, or act. For me, that's pretty much a daily battle.

When we do fall in these areas, we must simply admit our mistakes, examine why they happened, learn from them, and then determine to move forward in a different manner. With time and often after many attempts, we will overcome. And when we find ourselves in that place of victory, we will then be able to help others move forward as a result of the lessons we have learned.

Forget the Past and Move On

"Forget the former things; do not dwell on the past" (Isaiah 43:18 niv). For an athlete, dwelling on the former things, whether good or bad, could cause a delay in victory.

Countless experiences during my career on the water could have caused me to dwell on the past. As I've already mentioned, I've had falls galore. Sometimes even in the middle of a competitive run, I had to consciously shake off the past, learn from it, and press on. If I had focused on what went wrong or grieved over what could have been, or if I had wallowed in my sorrow, disappointment, or injustice, I would have missed what was still ahead—victory.

On the other hand, there were also many opportunities to rest on my laurels. It would have been so easy to focus on all my achievements and pat myself on the back, instead of continuing to move forward to even greater things. Becoming a champion required me to discipline my mind to stay focused on the goal of being the best I could be. I couldn't allow even my former victories to hinder my progress.

Spiritually speaking, this same concept is true. We cannot allow our defeats to cause us to wallow in self-pity and become overwhelmed with "if only" scenarios and "what if" questions. The past is the past. It can't be changed. There is nothing we can do but move forward and make better decisions in the future. It's true that some of our mistakes might have hurt people we love; it's also true that their mistakes might have greatly hurt us. Forgiveness is the key to being able to move forward.

On the flipside, we cannot allow our spiritual victories to cause us to settle in and become content in our relationship with God. A Christian walk is just that...a walk. It requires movement. If we are focused on our past relationship and victories with God, we will cease to move forward to our ultimate destinies.

FOCUS ON YOUR OWN PERFORMANCE

Before every competition, my father would tell me, "Go out there and beat Kristi. Don't worry about what those other girls are doing. Do what *you* can do." This was such great wisdom, and it caused me to constantly strive toward my potential.

When I did compare myself with other athletes, I was often tempted to hold back and do just enough to win. Conversely, when I focused on giving 100 percent of my effort as I took to the water then, whether I won or not, I returned to the dock without regrets.

Likewise, spiritually speaking, it's dangerous to compare our walk with Christ with that of someone else. Certainly we can look at someone's life and be spurred on by their commitment. We can even emulate the things they do that have led them to victory. But all in all, a relationship with God should be personal. We should strive to be all that God has called us to be, not who He has called someone else to be.

Here are some of the dangers of comparing ourselves to others spiritually:

First of all, we may become content if we discover we are further along in the knowledge of the Word than the person next to us. As a result, we may be tempted to give ourselves a pat on the back, even as we forfeit the opportunity to grow deeper in our personal relationship with God.

Secondly, we can become defeated if we look at someone's walk with God and wrongly reason that they know so much more about God than we do. We might be tempted to think that we are so far below where they are spiritually that we'll never get there.

Or, we may look at the way God is using someone else's life and think that our gifts must surely pale in comparison to theirs—how or why could God possibly use what we have. When we compare ourselves in this way, we run the risk of becoming jealous as we envy how God is working through someone else. In the end, we become so focused on wanting what they have that we fail to persevere in our own gifts.

We must realize that it's not about what other people are doing; it's about what God wants to do through each one of us, individually. It's about growing daily and using our God-given gifts for His glory. There are no insignificant people or gifts in God's eyes. We are all a vital part of His plan to reach a lost and dying world.

SET GOALS

I'm sure you've heard the saying, "If you aim at nothing, you'll hit nothing every single time."

As an athlete, I journeyed to the top of the podium because I continually set goals and pursued them wholeheartedly. Once I hit the target I was aiming for, I set my sights on a new one. This constant chasing after new goals kept me moving forward and prevented me from becoming stagnant.

Likewise, spiritual goals keep me from becoming spiritually stagnant. My ultimate goals are to know Christ more intimately each year and to glorify Him in all I say and do. Every January, I ask the Lord how He would have me move toward these goals. For me, they vary from year to year.

Some years He guides me to focus on developing my prayer life; other times He leads me to dive deeper into His Word. There have been times when I've felt led to join and even lead certain small groups, while other times He has drawn me away from people so that I can have more time to be still and listen to Him. Moving forward in these goals and being willing to change how I achieve them prevents me from merely going through the motions spiritually.

DON'T LOOK AT THE BUOYS

In the slalom event, I mastered the art of rounding obstacles instead of focusing on them. As I mentioned earlier, the slalom course is comprised of six buoys that the skier must successfully round. Early in my career, my parents taught me to gaze diagonally through the course instead of focusing on the upcoming buoys. It's a well-known fact that the moment the skier allows his or her eyes to zero in on those fast-approaching, little orange buoys, their run will come to an abrupt end.

It's simple: your body follows where your eyes are focused. If a skier wants to continue to move successfully through the course, he must refrain from looking at the buoys.

In life, we face obstacles too. They can appear in many forms—relational, financial, physical, emotional, or spiritual. The key to success, just as in slalom skiing, is to avoid focusing on the obstacles. We don't ignore them; rather, we fix our eyes on things above and give the obstacles to the Lord. With His help, we can round even the most difficult of life's buoys.

TAP INTO THE POWER SOURCE

I've mentioned several keys that can help anyone become a champion. (You can find a more comprehensive list with deeper explanations in my book, *Running the Course*.) Before I close this chapter, let me add one more thing: even with a focused mind, persevering heart, and teachable spirit, it's going to be hard for anyone to move forward to victory without being connected to a power source.

As a skier, the only way I could accomplish great feats on the water was by tapping into the incredible power source of the boat. Without it, I was going nowhere! I had huge biceps and a determined heart, but those two things alone weren't enough to move me forward to victory.

Similarly, the only way to accomplish great things—things with eternal value—is by choosing to be connected to God, the ultimate power source.

You may be wondering what that may look like. Here's a great example:

I am often asked to sing as well as speak at events, yet for years, I experienced incredible nerves before I sang. As I'd wait to take the stage, fear would overtake me, often leading to stomach pain, weakened knees, and dry mouth. During one such episode, I asked God to show me why I was experiencing these things. I could speak to crowds of thousands without fear. Why was singing so hard?

The Holy Spirit had a simple answer to my question, "You speak in My strength. You sing in yours."

He was right. When I spoke, I relied completely on the Lord. I didn't want anyone to hear my words. Instead, I wanted them to hear the very heart of God. Therefore, I invited God to take over, to speak through me, to anoint me with His power, and to encourage people with His life-giving truths.

But when I sang, I never thought about asking God to sing through me, to empower and anoint my voice to bring hope and healing to others. On the contrary, I only thought about pleasing those who listened. I chose songs I thought people would like to hear and that fit my voice so that I would sound good. Simply put, I sang for people, not God.

Once I learned to sing in God's strength, my music transformed. No longer was it just a performance—now it was a powerful tool the Holy Spirit used to penetrate the hearts of people with His love and truth. People would actually weep as the song ministered to their hearts and minds, just as they did when I spoke under His anointing. And you know what else? As I ministered in His strength, my fear disappeared.

God's strength is the most amazing thing I have ever experienced. It literally transforms me from the inside out, giving me supernatural power that enables me to do things that would be impossible if I was depending on myself.

Something to Think About

In the keys to victory just mentioned, there is a common theme of perseverance. Anyone who chooses to press through the disappointments and pain of their failures, with Christ at the helm, will ultimately live a victorious life.

The pain, however, isn't always easy to overcome. It can be difficult to live with the fact that our choices have hurt others. It's equally painful to face trials brought about by the actions of others—especially people we trusted and loved. Forgiveness is the key to moving forward during these painful times. It's really the only way.

When falls come, the first person we need to forgive is ourselves. Carrying around guilt and shame will hinder our victory.

Next, we must be willing to forgive those who have caused us pain—whether or not we feel they deserve to be forgiven and whether or not they have asked for it. Forgiveness isn't for our offenders; it's for us. Hanging on to an offense brings deadly consequences. I heard once: "Unforgiveness is like drinking poison and hoping the other person dies."

It's true. Unforgiveness tears apart businesses, families, friendships, churches, and ministries. It can even cause physical and mental sickness. The Bible warns that bitterness will defile many (Hebrews 12:15).

On the other hand, there will be times when we have to ask someone we've offended to forgive us. Then, if it's in our power, we need to make things right. This takes humility and courage.

Realize that sometimes the ones we have offended may be unwilling to forgive. That in itself is painful. The reality is that you can't control what someone else chooses to do. You can, however, choose to keep your heart pure and humble before God.

Many people will choose to stay in bitterness. My advice? Keep praying and leave your accusers in the hands of the Lord. He is the only One who can soften their hearts, open their eyes, and bring healing.

On many occasions, I've desperately wanted to step in and fix someone's heart, to do or say something that would ease their pain, or to help them understand the other side of the story (usually, my side). Yet as I've prayed, God has said, "Leave them with Me."

He has shown me that if I step in when He has told me to step aside, I can actually get in the way of someone's healing process. My words and actions, although backed by good intentions, can put a Band-Aid on someone's bleeding heart that God was looking to completely heal. The healing process often takes time and will lead that person through a journey that you can't control. Just keep praying.

As you forgive others and forgive yourself, as you ask God and others for forgiveness, and as you leave bitter hearts with God, you'll discover freedom. And with freedom comes the ability to move forward to victory. It puts you in a position to say "Hit it, God!" one more time.

CHAPTER 23

YOU CAN DO IT, BABY!

I can do everything through Christ, who gives me strength.
PHILIPPIANS 4:13

As I come to the end of this book, I find myself excited. Admittedly, I am overjoyed by the fact that this over two-year project has finally come to an end. But more so, I am excited about our family's future. At this particular moment, with a recent move to Central Florida under our ski vests, we find ourselves taking off from the starting dock of a new life journey, no doubt one that will be filled with lots of twists and turns.

For me, this book has served as a timely reminder that God is constantly behind the scenes of every aspect of our family's life. He is faithfully at work preparing the way and bringing about everything and everyone needed to accomplish His plans, from schools to friendships to connections that can help move the ministry forward. As I remember my adoption experiences, medical trials, and water-ski and ministry experiences, I know without a doubt that God will not fail us. I trust Him.

We go forth expectantly into this new adventure. God has placed many things on our hearts, and we are certain He will give birth to all of them in His perfect timing. Knowing this truth brings much peace to my heart.

Will I move forward perfectly? Most likely not. I'm sure my eager heart will lead me ahead of God, no matter how hard I try to contain myself. Just as in the past, falls will surely come in some shape or form, whether caused by my own choices or the choices of others.

Nevertheless, I am committed to move forward, to continue to learn, and to persistently say "Hit it, God!" every day of my life. I want to experience all that God has planned, and I know that God's victory will only come if I consistently follow Him.

Before you and I part ways, I'd like to share one final story from my water-ski career. I believe it will encourage your heart and spur you on to continually say "Hit it, God!" in your own life. This story comes from the 1999 World Championships in Milan, Italy.

Throughout my career, most victories came fairly quickly, though not without hard work. I won my first US Masters at the age of fifteen, broke the world record at twenty-two, and won every other event within a few tries…except for the World Championships. Over and over again, for some reason or another, that title kept eluding my grasp.

As I stood on the dock waiting to take my turn at the 1999 Worlds, I could only hope that this year would be different. As the top-seeded skier in the event, I took to the water knowing exactly what performance I needed to post. I skied well in my opening passes—a little more tentative than I would have liked but good enough to find myself in a position to win.

I rounded the first couple of buoys of the winning pass. Excitement mingled with fear began to rise up in my heart. I was almost there, just a single buoy away from victory! *Finally!*

I rounded that coveted fourth buoy—and stumbled. I watched in horror as the rope was violently snatched from my hands. Without warning, I found myself in a three-way tie for first place.

I sat in the water, overwhelmed with disbelief. Negative emotions and condemning thoughts began assaulting my heart and mind. "Way to go, Kristi. You screwed up again! You are such a failure and a disappointment to your family. They've done so much for you, spent so much money to be here, and once again, you failed." These and many other thoughts pounded away at my mind and eroded any hope I had of victory.

As I sat there wrestling with my thoughts, I heard something that changed my life forever. It was a voice—my father's Southern voice to be exact. I turned and looked toward the shoreline, and there he was, pushing his way through thousands of spectators to the water's edge.

He stepped into the water, yelling repeatedly at the top of his lungs, his fists pumping up into the air. "You can do it, baby!" He shouted. "You can do it, baby, you can do it!"

I have to admit it—at first I was a bit embarrassed as the boat crew looked at me in amazement and asked, "Is *that* your *father?*"

"Yep, that's my dad," I replied as I slid into the back of the boat and tried to ignore him.

Yet as the boat made its way to the end of the lake, I couldn't help but think about my father's words. They were backed with such power and emotion, such love. In the depths of his heart, my daddy knew that I was capable of overcoming this setback and coming home the victor.

I watched the other two girls fight their way through the course in our tie-breaker, and something new began to rise up in my heart. Hope! I was suddenly overwhelmed with the realization that it wasn't over. I still had a chance to win.

One by one, I captured my negative thoughts and replaced them with truth. "I *can* do this!" I encouraged myself as I began to shift my focus from my failure to the task that lay before me.

When the boat came back to the dock to pick me up, I chose to believe the words of my father. With a determined spirit, I gave the boat the command: "Hit it!"

Leaving my fear, anger, and self-pity on the dock, I took to the course with confidence and attacked every buoy with everything I had in me. And as a result, I came home the victor.

That experience radically changed my life.

No, there wasn't a huge check or a grand parade or a Wheaties commercial waiting for me when I returned home to the States. But there was a lesson, a revelation, that was forever engraved into my heart and mind.

Through the actions of my earthly father, I saw a beautiful picture of the intensity of God's love for me, His child. I saw His desire to spur me on to victory. To this day, I can close my eyes and see Daddy God, like my father, making His way into the water and yelling at the top of His lungs without a care as to who might hear. "You can do it, baby," He yells. "You can do it!"

I see Him ever so clearly, at every stage, running up and down the banks of my life, cheering me on to victory. And when I fall and find myself too weak, overwhelmed, or confused to get up again, I see Him swimming out, wrapping His arms around me, and climbing aboard those skis with me, infusing me with His very own strength, wisdom, peace, and joy.

It's the most beautiful sight in the world.

Can you see it? Can you see Him standing there, pumping His fists in victory, believing in you, loving you? Can you hear His voice of truth? Or are the voices of the world—your peers, your enemies, or your past mistakes—screaming so loudly that you cannot discern it?

My friend, God is calling out to you today. He's ready to take you on an adventure of a lifetime. Will you answer His call? Will you say "Hit it, God!" one more time?

Take it from me, your victory may just be one "hit it!" away!

With Christ, *you can do it, baby!*

As we come to the end of this final chapter, I can't stop smiling as I think back to this, my favorite story. What a fitting example of the theme of this book—the promise that our victory follows our willingness to say "Hit it!" and our decision to believe the words and trust the heart of our Heavenly Father.

It took years for me to obtain the title of world champion. Even in the example above, the day I finally brought home the gold, the victory didn't come easily. I had to fight for it. And I don't mean simply fight against my competition and tough conditions. More than anything, I had to fight against my own emotions and thoughts, both of which threatened to kill my hopes and dreams.

That was the real battle.

What if I'd swum to shore instead of grabbing hold of the rope and committing to go again? What if I'd let my thoughts overwhelm me and my own words condemn me? What if I hadn't believed my father's words of encouragement?

One thing is for sure, I would have never won the title of world champion.

Victory came only because of my willingness to try again, to risk it all, even failing and falling short once again.

The truth was this: when I committed to say "Hit it!" and give it one more shot, I didn't know if I'd come home the victor or not. I didn't know if my efforts would lead to one more disappointment or to the realization of my dreams.

But I was willing to take the chance, and because I did, victory came.

My friend, I don't know what dreams you are pressing toward or fighting for. Perhaps you have been waiting for the dream of a child, a spouse, financial provision, better health, a release from your current situation, or a restored relationship to come your way. Sometimes, like me, you may have found yourself in the water, just short of your dreams and desires and overwhelmed with negative emotions and stinkin' thinking!

Whatever you do—

Don't quit!

Don't stop pressing forward.

Don't stop dreaming and believing and hoping.

And whatever else you do—

Don't listen to those voices in your head or allow your emotions to rule your decisions.

Instead, listen to the voice of your Father calling out to you. Trust His heart and His love for you. Then stand on His Word and press on, committing to say "Hit it!" over and over and over again, until you stand on top of God's podium and hear the words, "Well done, good and faithful servant!"

I wish I could promise that the very next time you say those two little words will be the day you receive your victory, but I can't. What I can promise you, though, is this: it just might be. And even if it isn't, I guarantee you will be one step closer to standing in the realization of your dreams.

Just remember: you can't achieve victory if you aren't willing to push forward one more time.

So are you with me?

"Hit it!"

Something to Think About

For years I have had the privilege of sharing the message of "Hit it!" to thousands. Recently, as I was sharing this powerfully encouraging message with inmates in various Florida prisons and jails, I unexpectedly remembered a scene from my childhood.

I was about thirteen years old, getting ready to ski the waters of Lake Kristi for a large group of people. My father had invited friends from our church out to watch me practice. I remember looking up at all those people on the deck of our lake house and hoping it wouldn't fall into the water.

Bits of nerves began to run through my veins as the onlookers cheered. Nonetheless, I looked at the boat driver and said, "hit it!" as I had done a thousand times before. But just when I should have popped up out of the water, something pulled me back in. To my horror, I fell.

The crowd cheered me on. "You can do it!" they said in unison.

I wanted to sink under the water at the sound of their voices. I was so humiliated.

The boat came back to get me, and despite my embarrassing failure, I determined to say "hit it!" once again. The boat took off, and there it was again, an incredible force pulling me back into the water.

"Oh no, not again!" I thought.

With everything I had in me, I held on to the handle, barely rising up out of the water. Once I regained my composure, I realized what had happened. I was wearing a short-length wetsuit that was too big for my frame. Water had shot into the thigh area of the suit and filled it with pounds of water. The force of drag that had created had pulled me right back into the lake. As I looked behind me, I could see my normally thin rear-end jiggling with a load of water. It was not a pretty sight!

Knowing there was no way I would be able to successfully run the course with all that water sloshing about, I quickly grabbed hold of the bottom of my wetsuit and pulled it away from my skin. Water flowed down my leg. I was free! With the burden gone, I was again able to perform to the best of my ability.

With that scene fresh in my mind, I shared it with the inmates. Then I pointed out this powerful truth: even I, a determined professional skier, couldn't get out of the water carrying an extra burden of water weight. Regardless of how awesome and cutting edge my equipment, regardless of how powerful my boat, regardless of my determination to say "hit it!" and my desire to get up—I simply couldn't rise up.

The same is true in life. We can be ever so committed to say "hit it" to God. We can desire more than anything to be successful and to live victoriously. But if we are weighted down, we aren't going to get very far in our course.

We must be willing to open our hearts to God and allow the excess weight of anger, guilt, bitterness, jealousy, unforgiveness, self-pity, greed, and pride to flow out of our lives. We must release the cares and anxieties of our minds and let go of habits and sin that continually pull us back to the starting position.

No matter how hard we try, no matter how determined we are to say "hit it" to God, we must consistently "throw off all that entangles us" so that we can run the race He has set before us (Hebrews 12:1–3). Negative thoughts, emotions, and choices will inevitably weigh us down and prevent our victory. People, too, can be a hindrance.

What has you burdened and weighted down today? What are you holding on to that is keeping you from being victorious? Are you angry, bitter, or jealous? How about fearful, guilt-ridden, or ashamed? How are your relationships? It's time to grab the bottom of your wetsuit and let the water flow. It's time to lose the weight and be free!

CONCLUSION

When I reflect on how many times I must have said "Hit it!" to the boat driver during my water-ski career, I am amazed. But do you know what is even more amazing? It's how long it took me to say "Hit it!" to a Power Source that would never fail me or abandon me in the middle of the lake of life. A Power Source who has a plan and purpose for my life, who is never off course, and who loves me unconditionally.

From the time I was born, I had heard about this incredible Power Source, my God. I believed in His existence with all my heart. I also believed in His sacrifice, the giving of His Son's life for my salvation.

At the age of eight, I made a public profession of my faith in His Son, Jesus Christ, as my Savior. But do you know what? It took me twenty years from the time of my faith profession to make the decision to say "Hit it, God!" and to move out onto the waters of life with Him.

All those years, I was like a skier floating in the water, all hooked up to the boat yet going nowhere because of my unwillingness to trust the One at the controls. Truth be told, I had more faith in my ski boat than I did in the One who had laid down His life down for me. I also had more faith in my own ability and my resources to handle the issues of life than I did in the One who created me and the world.

I just wasn't willing to say "Hit it, God!" because I didn't trust Him or His plan for my life. Where would He take me? What would He ask me to give up? What would He expect me to do? Wouldn't He zap the fun out of life?

I didn't understand the depth of His love for me. I didn't understand the truth that out of His great love, He would take me on a journey that would bring the very things I had been searching for my entire life—joy, worth, peace, purpose, and satisfaction.

Because of this lack of knowledge, I continued to say "Hit it!" to the world, to people, and to my own desires—all things that brought temporary happiness at best—even while I was connected to God. Can you imagine holding on to two ski ropes connected to two different boats and yelling "Hit it"? Now that wouldn't be a pretty sight! It's the same thing spiritually. I couldn't move forward with God because I was trying to hang on to other power sources. In the end, I felt like I was being pulled apart.

I didn't understand my frustration. Like many people, I thought my belief in Jesus Christ's death, burial, and resurrection was all there was to being a Christian. I went to church. I prayed a couple of times a day. I read the Bible. I even gave God the credit for my victories. But I didn't realize that, although my faith in Jesus connected me to an incredible Power Source and brought me new life spiritually, I still had to say "Hit it, God!" in order to move forward with Him and to experience the abundant life Jesus had died to give me.

Just like the boat driver won't take off without the "hit it!" command, God doesn't take off unless we are willing to go with Him. He also will not go if we are still trying to hang on to other power sources.

I'm so thankful I finally made the decision to let go and let God lead the way. My life has never been the same. I can't say the waters have always been smooth. In fact, many obstacles have popped up along the way. Nor can I say my runs have been perfect. Many times I've strayed from the safety of His wakes.

But you know what? Without fail, God has been with me through the waters of difficulty. Time and time again, He gave me everything I needed to move forward to victory. And when I fell, He faithfully circled back, picked me up, and gave me another try.

Fortunately, I don't need calm waters for victory. Thankfully, God isn't looking for people who make perfect runs. God is simply looking for hearts that are willing to say "Hit it, God!" time and time again, no matter how rough the water, no matter how big the obstacle, no matter how hard the fall.

He's looking for a heart of perseverance, a heart willing to trust Him and move out into the unknown. Through that person, God can change the world.

Will you have that heart?

> *Dear Lord, today I make the decision to say "Hit it!" to You. More than anything, I want Your will for my life. Come into my heart. I accept Your free gift of salvation, given to me through the death of Your Son, Jesus. Not only do I trust you for my salvation, I trust You with my life. Today, I willingly give You access to my heart and mind. Use me, Lord. Give me courage and boldness to stand strong in my faith and a heart of perseverance to continually say "Hit it, God!" time and time again. Amen.*

If you prayed this prayer or have been challenged or inspired by this book, please visit **www.kojministries.com** and send me a note. I want to rejoice with you. Your testimony of faith spurs me on to continue to carry out the tasks God has placed on my heart.

From the time I was born in 1970, my favorite resting place was under the bow of our boat. The sound of the waves splashing against the fiberglass hull often lulled me to sleep.

Christmas morning of 1973 was exciting! Santa delivered a pair of water skis, a soda machine, and a new record player.

My best friend and training partner, Jackie, poses with me on my father's boat while waiting our turn to ski in 1974. Jackie and I trained together from 1974 to 1988.

I was so excited to be included in the "Who's Hot" feature of *Spray Magazine* in 1979. Photo courtesy of *Water Ski Magazine.*

Twisting and turning through my toe-pass as a junior competitor in
1982. Photo courtesy of *Water Ski Magazine.*

Running to meet my father after setting a junior national jump record at
the Southern Regionals Water Ski Championships in Alabama.

Soaring through the air on my Connelly jump skis in the early 1980s.
Due to my hip disorder, I eventually retired from jump and trick events
and became a slalom specialist. Photo courtesy of *Water Ski Magazine.*

Upon returning home from my first US Masters Water Ski Tournament
win in 1985, I was welcomed at the airport by my family, friends, and a
local television crew.

With my family in Milan, Italy, at the opening ceremonies of the 1985
Junior World Championships.

Tim shows off his skills in 1990. It was on this very board that he
completed a wake-to-wake 360 degree turn, which earned him a dinner
date with me.

Just married, Tim and I walk to our wedding reception at Lake Kristi.
(July 24, 1994)

An aerial photo of Lake Kristi during the US Open Water Ski
Championships. We hosted this international event in 1996 and 1997.

Cover shot of *Water Ski Magazine*, March 1999. Reproduced with
permission of *Water Ski Magazine*.

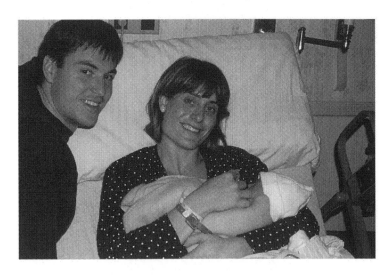

Tim and I welcomed our little one, Tymothy (Ty) Parker Johnson, on
December 12, 1997. Just eleven weeks later, all three of us were on a plane
heading to Australia, so I could compete in the Moomba Masters.

Tim and I celebrating our slalom win at the 1999 World Championships in Milan, Italy.

Waving to the crowd at the 1999 World Championships in Milan, Italy. Photo by Ross Outerbridge.

Ty riding with me in the Parade of Champions Opening Ceremony at the US Masters Water Ski and Wake Board Tournament in 2002.

This is one of my favorite photographs that captures the beauty and challenge of Robin Lake at Callaway Gardens. Competing on Robin Lake at the US Masters Water Ski and Wake Board Tournament during 1983-2009 provided many memories and lessons.

In 2003, In His Wakes was founded. These children from Greenville, North Carolina, were the first participants in our "A Day to Remember" program. Thousands of lives have since been impacted through the outreach of this unique nonprofit organization.

Ivy and I share a special ride on a tube with Twinkles, a 2013 participant of the In His Wakes D2R program held at Lake Kristi.

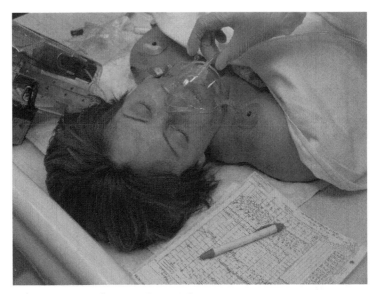

In recovery after my first pelvic reconstructive surgery in
Boston in January 2004.

Playing with Dalton and Ivy at the Russian orphanage, just days before
our adoption in April 2005.

Our first night at our Florida home together in 2005. I can only imagine what these two little Russian chatterboxes were thinking as I read to them. Ty was so happy to have his mommy back home after such a long trip away.

The Johnsons pose for our first family photo.
Photo by Amy Barry, May 2005.

Tim and I met Todd and Bonnie Hagemann and their two children in 2006 at an In His Wakes event in Missouri. We experienced an immediate bond as parents of two precious siblings, Dalton (Denis) and Joel (Misha).

Witnessing God reunite Dalton (Denis) and Joel (Misha) was incredible. The brothers had not seen each other since being adopted from Russia. God is indeed a miracle-working God! The Johnson and Hagemann children quickly bonded and are closest of friends. Pictured are Ty, Erin, Dalton, Joel and Ivy in 2006.

No one was more surprised than I to find myself competing at the 2007
World Championships in Linz, Austria.

Nothing brings me more joy than encouraging and mentoring people. Here,
I am presenting world-class water-skier Anna Gay with a special award at the
US Masters Water Ski and Wake Board awards banquet in 2012.

Director Nate Miller and I had the privilege of baptizing this young man
at Lake Kristi during an In His Wakes event.

Having some fun in Arizona at a friend's annual Pumpkin Ski
Competition in 2010.

It's always a privilege to visit my mentor, Ralph Meloon, a founder of Correct Craft Boats. Even in his upper 90s, Mr. Ralph still goes into the office. In 2011, I visited Mr. Ralph at work with my dear friend, Margarita Oganisyan. Margarita and her family were instrumental in our Russian adoption process and have become like family to us.

WNCT-TV sports director and longtime friend, Brian Bailey, interviewing my father and me prior to my North Carolina Sports Hall of Fame induction in May 2012.

In 2013, I returned to Russia with gifts for the orphanage where my children once lived. In this photograph, I am sharing pictures of Dalton and Ivy with the ladies who'd raised them.

Ivy meeting her biological brother, Nikita, and his foster sister, Sonia, in Russia. (2014)

Tim poses with his mother, Pav, after coaching Ty's high school football team to a state championship victory. Tim is a great coach both on and off the water. Photo taken 2013.

Lifelong friends, Kyle and Hope Tate, celebrate my induction into the USA Water Ski Hall of Fame in 2013. Kyle's coaching techniques helped me climb to the top of the podium.

Celebrating Christmas 2013 with my parents at their home with my brother Michael, his wife Holly, and their children.

Visiting with Bill Doyle in the Miami Federal Prison in August 2013. God used Bill in a powerful way to prepare my heart for prison ministry.

Speaking to a group of incarcerated women at Gadsden Correctional Institution in 2014. You should have seen these ladies learning to water-ski on dry land! We had a blast.

2014 Johnson Family Christmas photo. Our family's mission is to do justly, love mercy, and walk humbly before our God.
Photo by Geri Simpkins.

A CHALLENGE FOR YOU

They have defeated him by the blood of the
Lamb and by their testimony.
And they did not love their lives so much
that they were afraid to die.
REVELATION 12:11

The Word of God says that the enemy is overcome by the word of our testimony and by the blood of the Lamb. I believe that as Christians we have
a responsibility to share the incredible, redemptive power of God so that
others can know Him in a real and personal way and so that the bondage
that enslaves so many can be broken.

Satan knows there is power in our testimonies, in our life stories. That's
why he works so very hard to keep us silent, telling us that no one needs
to know that part of our life. He tries to convince us to wear a mask and
pretend that all is okay. He even goes so far as to convince us that we don't
even have a testimony worth sharing.

You've just read my story. Now, I challenge you to share yours. Anyone
who has truly given their lives to Christ has a story, and your story has the
power to radically change someone's life. It can give hope, encouragement,
or maybe even the good ole kick in the rear that someone else needs to
move forward in life.

If you feel led to share your story, would you consider submitting it to
KOJM for possible inclusion in our life-changing publication, *Victorious
Living*? God is using *Victorious Living* to touch many hearts around the
nation and internationally.

Right now, you may be thinking, *but I can't write!* That's okay. We
have wonderful writers who can take your words and powerfully arrange

them to bring God the glory. All you need is a heart willing to share your story of God's faithfulness. He will take care of the rest.

You can submit your story online at www.kojministries.org. Please note:

- Submissions are not guaranteed to be included in magazine.
- Submission is acknowledgement of your granting KOJM and Victorious Living Publications the rights to produce your submission in magazine and other ministry publications.
- Photos submitted must have the photographer's and the photographed subject's consent of reproduction.
- Photographer's name must be included. Hard copies of photographs will not be returned.
- *Victorious Living* does not pay for submissions.
- Submissions should be a maximum of eight hundred words and are subject to editing.

About the Author

As a professional water-skier for over twenty years and the world record holder in women's slalom from 1992 to 2010, **Kristi Overton Johnson** took to the waters of the world with passion, perseverance, and a desire to impact the world of water-skiing. This wife and mother of three now focuses her passions and gifts to encourage people to run the course of life victoriously.

Kristi married best friend Tim Johnson in 1994. Kristi and Tim met while attending the University of Central Florida. Upon graduating, they attended the University of Florida College of Law, where they received their Juris Doctorates and licenses to practice law. They have three children, the youngest two adopted from Russia in 2005. They currently live in Florida, home base of Kristi Overton Johnson Ministries.

Kristi is a sought after, faith-based motivational speaker who has a remarkable ability to encourage hearts in an exciting way through analogies from her life experiences. She has spoken across the country as well as internationally. If you are interested in Kristi coming to speak at your function, contact BookKristi@kojministries.org.

Professional Skiing Career

A native of Greenville, North Carolina, Kristi began her competitive water-ski career at age five on the shores of the Pamlico River in Bath. With the help of her Lord, family, friends, and sponsors, Kristi captured state, regional, and national records in the slalom, trick, and jump events before turning professional at the tender age of thirteen.

Although a Master's champion and number-one world ranked athlete in the trick event, Kristi began to specialize in the slalom event in 1988 due to a congenital hip deformity. For fifteen years, Kristi dominated the women's slalom event, accumulating eighty professional wins and capturing more number-one world rankings than any other female skier in history. She is an eight-time US Masters Champion, and a four-time US Open Champion. She held the world record in women's slalom from 1992–2010.

Kristi traveled the world, bringing home the gold and setting records as a World Champion, Pan American Games, and US Pro Tour Champion. She won the British, French, Italian, Australian, and Austrian Masters. She was inducted into the North Carolina Sports Hall of Fame in May 2012 and the USA Water Ski Hall of Fame in 2013.

Kristi departed the professional circuit in 2004 after several major surgeries, including a complete reconstruction of her pelvis. She made a brief appearance back on the water at the 2007 and 2009 World Championships, as well as the 2008 and 2009 US Masters Water Ski and Wakeboard Tournaments. After going through another series of medical trials, Kristi stepped away once again from competition.

Kristi is still very active in the sport of water-skiing. She mentors and coaches young athletes, provides scholarships, and introduces people to the sport of water-skiing and her Lord through **IN HIS WAKES**, an international water-sports ministry that Kristi founded in 2003.

MINISTRIES FOUNDED BY
KRISTI OVERTON JOHNSON

IN HIS WAKES

With a passion to share the life lessons she learned on the water and a desire to encourage the hearts of people through her faith, Kristi founded **In His Wakes**, a nonprofit organization, in 2003. In His Wakes has helped thousands of at-risk youth from across the nation and the world gain hope, experience victory, and discover their purpose through the sport that brought Kristi fame. The mission of In His Wakes is to introduce people to the life-changing power of Jesus Christ through water sports. For more information, visit **www.inhiswakes.com.**

KRISTI OVERTON JOHNSON MINISTRIES

In 2009, Kristi founded the nonprofit organization, **Kristi Overton Johnson Ministries.** Through its publications, speaking/teaching/singing ministry, and prison and international orphanage outreaches, KOJM pierces the heart of captives. KOJM seeks to evangelize the gospel of Jesus Christ by equipping minds and encouraging hearts with the Living Water of God's Word.

For current contact information about the above outreaches of KOJM, visit **www.kojministries.org.**

We invite you to partner with us through your prayers, volunteer support, and financial partnership. Together, we can encourage hearts and equip minds with the love of Christ.

75440859R00131

Made in the USA
Columbia, SC
21 August 2017